THE ERRORS C

AN ARGUMENT

DELIVERED IN THE

REPRESENTATIVES' HALL, BOSTON,

APRIL 3, 1867,

BEFORE A

JOINT SPECIAL COMMITTEE OF THE GENERAL
COURT OF MASSACHUSETTS.

By JOHN A. ANDREW.

BOSTON:

TICKNOR AND FIELDS.

1867.

WRIGHT & POTTER, PRINTERS, 4 SPRING LANE.

THE ERRORS OF PROHIBITION.

AN ARGUMENT

DELIVERED IN THE

REPRESENTATIVES' HALL, BOSTON,

APRIL 3, 1867,

BEFORE A

JOINT SPECIAL COMMITTEE OF THE GENERAL COURT OF MASSACHUSETTS.

By JOHN A. ANDREW.

BOSTON:
TICKNOR & FIELDS, 124 TREMONT ST
1867.

INTRODUCTORY.

At the present annual session of the General Court of Massachusetts, commencing in January, 1867, petitions were presented by Alpheus Hardy and others, praying for enactment of a judicious license law for the regulation and control of the sale of spirituous and fermented liquors in the Commonwealth. The number of these Petitioners during the session already (April, 1867,) comprises thirty thousand legal voters, and is increasing daily.

A petition was also presented by the principal inn-keepers in the city of Boston, praying for such changes in existing laws concerning the sale of wines and liquors as shall allow them to supply the wants of the guests of their houses, yet under such excise and regulation and subject to such supervision as shall be deemed needful for the public good.

A further petition was presented by the officers and trustees of the Massachusetts College of Pharmacy, representing that under the present statutes it is impossible legally to conduct that business and perform its duties to the medical profession and the sick, and praying for such amendment of the law as that apothecaries may be enabled to conduct their business in a legal manner.

Various petitions, numerously signed, were also presented to the General Court, remonstrating against any amendment of the existing prohibitory statutes.

All these petitions were referred to a Joint Special Committee of the two branches of the legislature, composed of

Messrs. MORSE, of Norfolk,
ALEXANDER, of Hampden,
FAY, of Suffolk,
DOW, of Middlesex,
SWAN, of Bristol,
On the part of the Senate; and

Messrs. JEWELL, of Boston,
ALDRICH, of Worcester,
SHERMAN, of Lowell,
WRIGHT, of Lawrence,
AVERY, of Braintree,
FLINN, of Chatham,
McCLELLAN, of Grafton,
BARTLETT, of Roxbury,
MADDEN, of Boston,
On the part of the House of Representatives.

The Petitioners were represented before the Committee by Hon. John A. Andrew and Hon. Linus Child, as counsel; and the Remonstrants were in like manner represented before the Committee by Hon. Asahel Huntington, Rev. A. A. Miner, D. D., and William B. Spooner, Esq., as counsel.

The hearings were continued for four days in each week, (besides two evening sessions,) beginning February 19th, and ending April 3d, at first in the Senate Chamber, and afterwards in the Representatives' Hall, in the State House, at Boston.

The opening argument for the Petitioners was made by Hon. LINUS CHILD, and the following witnesses were called, sworn and examined in their behalf:—

John Q. Adams, Esq., of Quincy,
(Trial Justice for Norfolk County.)

Rev. Nehemiah Adams, D. D., of Boston.

Prof. Louis Agassiz, of Cambridge,
(Prof. of Zoölogy and Geology in the Scientific School of Harvard College.)

Rev. William R. Alger, of Boston.

Joseph Andrews, Esq., of Boston.

Rev. Leonard Bacon, D. D., of New Haven, Conn.,
(Professor of Didactic Theology in Yale College.)

Rev. Charles F. Barnard, of Boston.

Dr. George F. Bigelow, of Boston,
(Secretary of the Howard Benevolent Association, and Physician at the Washingtonian Home.)

Prof. Henry J. Bigelow, M. D., of Boston,
(Professor of Surgery in the Medical School of Harvard College.)

Hon. Henry W. Bishop, of Lenox,
(Ex-Judge of the Court of Common Pleas.)

Rev. George W. Blagden, D. D., of Boston,
(Senior Pastor of the Old South Church.)

Hon. J. C. Blaisdell, of Fall River.

Rev. John A. Bolles, D. D., of Boston,
(Rector of the Church of the Advent.)

Prof. Francis Bowen, of Cambridge,
(Alford Professor of Natural Theology, Moral Philosophy and Civil Polity in Harvard College.)

Rev. Robert Brady, of Boston,
(Pastor of St. Mary's Church.)

Augustus O. Brewster, Esq., of Boston,
(Ex-Assistant District-Attorney for Suffolk County.)

A. M. Brownell, Esq., of New Bedford,
(Municipal Marshal of that city.)

Hon. E. P. Buffington, of Fall River,
(Ex-Mayor of that city.)

Brigadier-General Isaac S. Burrell, of Roxbury,
(Ex-Municipal Marshal of that city.)

Rev. B. F. Clark, of Chelmsford.

Prof. Edward H. Clarke, M. D., of Boston,
(Professor of Materia Medica in the Medical School of Harvard College.)

Hon. John H. Clifford, of New Bedford,
(Ex-Governor and Ex-Attorney-General of the Commonwealth.)

John C. Cluer, Esq., of Boston.

Hon. Charles G. Davis, of Plymouth.

E. Hasket Derby, Esq., of Boston.

Rev. Manassas Doherty, of Cambridge.

Hon. J. H. Duncan, of Haverhill.

Right Rev. Manton Eastburn, D. D., of Boston,
(Bishop of the Protestant Episcopal Church of the Diocese of Massachusetts.)

Frank Edson, Esq., of Hadley,
(Chairman of the Selectmen and Liquor Agent of that town.)

Rev. Theodore Edson, D. D., of Lowell.

Rev. George E. Ellis, D. D., of Charlestown.

Rev. Rufus Ellis, of Boston.

M. J. Fassin, Esq., of New York.

Hon. Francis B. Fay, of Lancaster,
(Ex-Mayor of Chelsea, and Trustee of the State Reform School for Girls at Lancaster.)

Hon. Henry F. French, of Cambridge,
(Ex-Assistant-District-Attorney for Suffolk County.)

Addison Gage, Esq., of West Cambridge.

Thomas Gaffield, Esq., of Boston.

Hon. E. B. Gillette, of Westfield,
(District-Attorney for the Western District.)

Albert G. Goodwin, Esq.,
(Secretary of the Boston Provident Association.)

Hon. Alpheus Hardy, of Boston.

Benjamin W. Harris, Esq., of Milton,
(Ex-District-Attorney for the South-Eastern District.)

Rev. Michael Hartney, of Salem.

Rev. George F. Haskins, of Boston,
(Head of the House of the Angel Guardian.)

Rev. James A. Healey, of Boston.

Rev. Frederick H. Hedge, D. D., of Brookline,
(Prof. of Ecclesiastical History in the Divinity School of Harvard College.)

Henry Hill, Esq., of Braintree.

Hon. George S. Hillard, of Boston,
(United States District-Attorney for the District of Massachusetts.)

Prof. Oliver Wendell Holmes, M. D., of Boston,
(Parkman Professor of Anatomy and Physiology in the Medical School of Harvard College.)

Prof. E. N. Horsford, of Cambridge,
(Ex-Rumford Professor of the Application of Science to the Art of Life in the Scientific School of Harvard College.)

Capt. David Hoyt, of Deerfield.

Rev. G. B. Ide, D. D., of Springfield.

Prof. Charles T. Jackson, M. D., of Boston.

Prof. J. B. S. Jackson, M. D., of Boston,
(Shattuck Professor of Morbid Anatomy in the Medical School of Harvard College.)

Rev. John Jones, of Pelham.

Col. John Kurtz, of Boston,
(Chief of Police of the city.)

Wm. M. Lathrop, Esq., of Boston.

Rev. Thomas R. Lambert, of Charlestown.

Louis Lapham, Esq., of Fall River,
(Judge of the Police Court of that city.)

Hon. George Lewis, of Roxbury,
(Mayor of that city.)

Hon. D. Waldo Lincoln, of Worcester,
(Ex-Mayor of that city.)

Hon. Frederic W. Lincoln, Jr., of Boston,
(Ex-Mayor of the city.)

Rev. Increase S. Lincoln, of Warwick.

Rev. Samuel K. Lothrop, D. D., of Boston.

Rev. J. C. Lovejoy, of Cambridge.

Hon. Alfred Macy, of Nantucket.

enry A. Marsh, Esq., of Amherst.

Samuel F. McCleary, Esq., of Boston,
(City Clerk.)

Rev. Lawrence McMahon, of New Bedford.

Hon. William S. Messervy, of Salem,
(Ex-Mayor of that city.)

Rev. Rollin H. Neale, D. D., of Boston.

Lyman Nichols, Esq., of Boston.

Hon. Otis Norcross, of Boston,
(Mayor of the city.)

Rev. J. B. O'Hagan, of Boston.

P. L. Page, Esq., of Pittsfield,
(Judge of the Police Court of that town.)

Hon. Henry W. Paine, of Cambridge.

Hon. John C. Park, of Boston.

Charles Henry Parker, Esq., of Boston,
(Manager of the Suffolk Institution for Savings.)

Hon. Joel Parker, of Cambridge,
(Royall Professor in the Law School of Harvard College; formerly Chief Justice of the Supreme Court of the State of New Hampshire.)

E. B. Patch, Esq., of Lowell.

Prof. Andrew P. Peabody, D. D., LL. D., of Cambridge,
(Preacher to the University, and Plummer Professor of Christian Doctrine and Morals in Harvard College.)

Hon. J. H. Perry, of New Bedford,
(Mayor of that city.)

Chase Philbrick, Esq., of Lawrence,
(Municipal Marshal of that city.)

Edward L. Pierce, Esq., of Milton,
(District-Attorney for the South-Eastern District.)

Rev. John Power, of Worcester.

Rev. George Putnam, D. D., of Roxbury.

Hon. George C. Richardson, of Cambridge,
(Ex-Mayor of that city; Pres. of the Board of Trade of the city of Boston.)

Rev. John P. Robinson, of Boston.

Hon. Charles Russell, of Princeton.

Hon. Charles Theodore Russell, of Cambridge,
(Ex-Mayor of that city.)

Hon. George P. Sanger, of Boston,
(District-Attorney for Suffolk County.)

Edward A. Savage, Esq., of Boston,
(Deputy-Chief of Police of the city.)

Rev. Thomas Shehan, of Taunton.

J. E. Souchard, Esq., French Consul at Boston.

Oliver Stackpole, Esq., of Boston.

Prof. D. Humphreys Storer, M. D., of Boston,
(Professor of Obstetrics and of Medical Jurisprudence in the Medical School of Harvard College.)

Rev. Patrick Strain, of Lynn.

Rev. Edward T. Taylor, D. D., of Boston,
(Pastor at the Seamens' Bethel in that city.)

Minot Tirrell, Jr., Esq., of Lynn.

Rev. John Todd, D. D., of Pittsfield.

Rev. John E. Todd, of Boston.

Rev. Joseph Tracy, D. D., of Beverly,
(Lately Editor of the Boston Recorder.)

Hon. George B. Upton, of Boston.

Theodore Voelckers, Esq., of Boston.

Hon. G. Washington Warren, of Charlestown,
(Judge of the Police Court, and Ex-Mayor of that city.)

Hon. Emory Washburn, of Cambridge,
(Bussey Professor in the Law School of Harvard College; Ex-Governor of the Commonwealth; and formerly Judge of the Court of Common Pleas.)

Rev. E. M. P. Wells, of Boston,
(Rector of St. Stephen's Church.)

Prof. James C. White, M. D., of Boston,
(Assistant-Professor of Chemistry in Harvard College.)

H. W. B. Wightman, Esq., of Chelmsford,
(Treasurer of the Chelmsford Foundry Company.)

Hon. Joseph M. Wightman, of Boston,
(Ex-Mayor of the city.)

Rev. Thomas Worcester, D. D., of Boston.

In support of the petition of the College of Pharmacy, which was represented by Messrs. Thomas Hollis, President, Samuel M. Colcord, Vice-President, and Henry W. Lincoln, Recording Secretary, as a special committee of its Board of Trustees, the following gentlemen appeared as witnesses :—

Charles Edward Buckingham, M. D.,
(Surgeon of City Hospital, Boston.)

Charles C. Bixby, of North Bridgewater,
(Apothecary.)

Isaac T. Campbell, of Boston,
(Examiner of Drugs.)

S. M. Colcord, of Boston, Apothecary,
(Vice-President of Massachusetts College of Pharmacy.)

Thomas Hollis, Apothecary, Boston,
(President of the Massachusetts College of Pharmacy.)

James L. Hunt, Apothecary,
(Town Liquor Agent of Hingham.)

Henry W. Lincoln, Apothecary, Boston,
(Recording Secretary of Massachusetts College of Pharmacy.)

William T. Rand, Dedham,
(Formerly an apothecary.)

Sampson Reed, Druggist,
(Formerly an Alderman of Boston.)

Frank W. Simmons, Apothecary, Boston,

2

10

The opening argument for the Remonstrants was then made by Hon. Asahel Huntington, who was followed by William B. Spooner, Esq., and after the examination of their witnesses, the Rev. A. A. Miner, on Tuesday, April 2d, delivered the closing argument in their behalf. He was followed, on Wednesday, April 3, by Hon. John A. Andrew, in behalf of the Petitioners, who closed the hearing with the following

ARGUMENT.

Mr. Chairman and Gentlemen of the Committee:—

A measure so extreme and unusual as the statute of Massachusetts—prohibiting the sale of spirituous and fermented liquors, notwithstanding that they are confessedly commercial articles—can rest only on some proposition in science or morals of corresponding sweep. And, although our legislation is not entirely consistent in its details with any theory, yet it does in fact rest on a theory which involves these two positions, viz.: *The essentially poisonous character of alcoholic beverages*, and *The immorality of their use.* It assumes that any law which permits (and regulates) their sale is "immoral and an educator of immorality." *

I.

The advocates of Prohibition base their argument in part upon the assumption that alcohol is a poison, in the sense in which strychnine or arsenic is poison, to be administered to the human system only

---

* Minority Report of 1866, House Document 359, p. 33.

*under the restrictions applicable to the administra-
tion of fatal drugs.*

They affirm this of alcohol taken in whatever
doses, averring, as it has been concisely expressed
by another, "*that whatever is true of the excessive
use of alcohol is true also in proportionate degree
of the moderate and occasional use.*" Dr. Carpenter, Registrar of the University of London, and
the leading scientific authority with the advocates
of prohibition, declares in set terms that "*The
action of Alcohol upon the animal body in health
is essentially poisonous.*"

Let us therefore at the outset investigate this
assumption that alcohol is necessarily a *poison*,
with an eye to see, (in the language of Liebig
concerning tea and coffee, substances akin to,
though differing somewhat from, alcohol in their
working on the human frame,) "whether it depend
on sensual and sinful inclinations merely that every
people of the globe has appropriated some such
means of acting on the nervous life." *

Twenty years ago alimentary substances were
classified by Liebig as Respiratory Food, and as
Plastic Food, the line of distinction between them,
in composition, being the absence or presence of

* Liebig's Letters on Chemistry, 3d London edition, p. 456.

nitrogen, and the line of distinction between them in their transformation in the human body, being according to Liebig's theory, that though both are burned by the inhaled oxygen, yet the former is burned directly by it, without previous transformation into the human tissues, while part of the latter, before final consumption,' becomes human tissue.

Concisely stated, Liebig's two classes of food are, therefore,

I. Certain non-azotized substances, which, from their large amount of carbon, serve (as fuel,) to keep up the animal heat, and which he names *the elements of respiration.*

II. Certain nitrogenized substances, which are adapted to the formation of blood, (out of that, muscle, and the tissues,) and which he terms *the plastic elements of nutrition.*

Liebig's theory of combustion or oxidation, and the sharpness of his distinction between his classes, have been modified by recent scientific disputants; but his position that alcoholic beverages taken in fit combinations, and in due moderation, perform the functions of food, remains unshaken.

˙He says,—

" Besides fat and those substances which contain carbon
and the elements of water, man consumes, in the shape of
the alcohol of fermented liquors, another substance, which
in his body, plays exactly the same part as the non-nitrogenized constituents of food.

" The alcohol, taken in the form of wine or any other
similar beverage, disappears in the body of man. Although
the elements of alcohol do not possess by themselves the
property of combining with oxygen at the temperature of
the body, and forming carbonic acid and water, yet alcohol
acquires, by contact with bodies in the condition of erema-
causis or absorption of oxygen, such as are invariably present in the body, this property to a far higher degree than is
known to occur in the case of fat and other non-nitrogenized
substances." *

Not only have many physiologists and chemists
adopted this general theory, but even those others,
who modify the theory of Liebig as stated by
himself, nevertheless classify alcoholic drinks in
the category of foods.†

* Animal Chemistry, 3d edition: London. pp. 97, 98.
† See, among other authorities, *Clinical Medicine*, by W. T. Gairdner,
Physician to the Royal Infirmary of Edinburgh, and Lecturer on the
Practice of Medicine; and Human Physiology, Statical and Dynamical;
or, the Conditions and Course of the Life of Man, by Prof. John W.
Draper, pp. 27, 28.

See, also, the Boston Medical and Surgical Journal, for January 31,
1867, which contains a brief account of Dr. Frankland's deductions from
his own experiments and those of Professors Fick and Wislicenus, concerning the capacity of non-azotized food to supply power and repair
waste.

15

In the result which we shall reach concerning alcohol, it makes no practical difference whether Liebig's division of food stands or falls. If alcohol be food, it matters not to the question of a Prohibitory Law, whether it be Respiratory Food or Plastic Food.

Dr. Carpenter himself, admits alcohol, in one work,* into the category of foods, classifying it with the oleaginous group of foods, although in another work,† denouncing it as *poison*. As Mr. Lewes tersely says of him on just this point:— " We have only to disentangle his confusion and we find him an ally."

Alcohol contains the carbon and hydrogen which belong to the normal elements of the body, and *common experience* in all wine-growing and beer-drinking countries, and the experience of invalids and convalescents everywhere, who are often supported almost entirely on alcoholic fluids, show that they are assimilated. Therefore (though not proper, undiluted, any more than saltpetre, or oxygen are good food by themselves,) it is capable of acting, and does act, in certain beverages, as a food.

* Human Physiology, p. 475.
† Physiology of Temperance and Total Abstinence.

16

That light wines, ale, beer and cider act (when moderately used,) as a poison, is contradicted also by *common experience*, by examples like the life-long practice of Cornaro, and the testimony of entire nations and successive ages.

Cornaro from his fortieth year to his death, restricted himself to a daily allowance of twelve ounces of solid food and fourteen ounces of wine. Of him Dr. Carpenter writes:*—

" The smallest quantity of food upon which life is known to have been supported with vigor during a prolonged period, is that on which Cornaro states himself to have subsisted. This was no more than twelve ounces a day chiefly of vegetable matter, with fourteen ounces of light wine, for a period of fifty-eight years." Born at Venice in 1467, he died at Padua in 1566.

Commenting upon this statement by Dr. Carpenter, Mr. George Henry Lewes, (author of the Physiology of Common Life,) says:†—" Observe the proportion of wine in this diet, and then ask how it is in the face of such facts, that Dr. Carpenter can deny the nutritive value of alcohol."

Concerning wine Liebig says:—‡

* Human Physiology, p. 387.
† Westminster Review, No. cxxv., July, 1855.
‡ Letters on Chemistry, 3d London edition, p. 454.

" As a restorative, a means of refreshment when the powers of life are exhausted, of giving animation and energy where man has to struggle with days of sorrow, *as a means of correction and compensation where misproportion occurs in nutrition*, wine is surpassed by no product of nature or of art. * * * In no part of Germany do the apothecaries' establishments bring so low a price as in the rich cities on the Rhine ; for there wine is the universal medicine of the healthy as well as the sick. It is considered as milk for the aged."

Pereira writes as follows concerning beer:—

."Considered dietetically, beer possesses a threefold property ; it quenches thirst; it stimulates, cheers, and if taken in sufficient quantity, intoxicates; lastly, it nourishes or strengthens. * * * Beer proves a refreshing and salubrious drink (if taken in moderation,) and an agreeable and valuable stimulus and support to those who have to undergo much bodily fatigue."

In the article " Diet," in Chambers's Encyclopædia,* the writer says :—

" The laboring man, who can hardly find bread and meat enough to preserve the balance between the formation and decay of his tissues, finds in alcohol an agent which, if taken in moderation, enables him, without disturbing his health, to dispense with a certain quantity of food, and yet keeps up the weight and strength of his body."

* Chambers's Encyclopædia, Vol. iii., p. 552. Art. Diet. See also the Anatomy of Drunkenness, by Dr. Macnish, p. 225.

3

Nay, at the close of Dr. Carpenter's work on the Physiology of Temperance and Total Abstinence,—a work which is the scientific manual of the Prohibitionists,—occurs the following passage. He is arguing upon a thesis which he expresses as follows, viz.: that "whilst the habitual use of alcoholic liquors, even in the most moderate amount, is likely, (except in a few rare cases,) to be injurious, great benefit may be derived in the treatment of *disease*, from the medicinal use of alcohol in appropriate cases." And he comes finally to speak of "a class of individuals, who," he says, "can scarcely be regarded as subjects of disease, but in whom the conditions are essentially different from those of health." "These are such," he continues, "as, from constitutional debility, or early habits, or some other cause that does not admit of rectification, labor under an habitual deficiency of appetite and digestive power, even when they are living under circumstances generally most favorable to vigor, and when there is no indication of disordered action in any organ, all that is needed being a slight increase in the capacity for preparing the aliment which the body really needs. Experience affords ample evidence that there *are* such cases, especially among those engaged in avocations which involve a good deal of mental activity; and that, *with* the assistance of a small but habitual allowance of alcoholic stimulants, a long life of active exertion may be sustained, whilst the vital powers would speedily fail *without* their aid, not for the want of direct support from them, but for the want of the measure of food which the system really needs, and which no other means seems so effectual in enabling it to appropriate. * * * To withhold the assistance of alcoholic stimulants, (it is in their very mildest form, such as that of bitter ale, that they are most beneficial,) would often be to condemn the individuals in question to a life-long debility, incapacitating them from all activity of exertion in behalf of themselves or others, and rendering them susceptible to a variety of other causes of disease. For it seems to be the peculiar character of this condition, that no other medicine can supply what is wanting, with the same effect as a small quantity of an alcoholic beverage, taken with the principal meal of the day."

This extract, from Carpenter, leads us to consider now, *what is a stimulant?* It is often alleged against alcohol that it is stimulating; that it is even more stimulating than almost any other substance in ordinary use for diet. But what is a stimulant? Is a substance intrinsically deleterious for diet because it is stimulating? Is it justly a reproach to a man that he uses stimulants? Let us not be deceived by *words*. Let us probe.this question. And first, for a brief, clear, sharp, incisive definition of the term "stimulant." This has been well expressed thus:—

"Stimu*lants* are only energetic stimu*li*. Now all living acts require stimuli,—the eye light, the egg and seed heat or heat and moisture, the stomach food, sometimes condiments. It is hard to draw the line. Ninon de l'Enclos said her soup made her tipsy, and convalescents have been said to get drunk on a beefsteak. That which is a stimu*lus* to one person is a stimu*lant* to another. The last term means only a more concentrated form of stimulus, or one which acts more vigorously than ordinary stimuli, for any reason in itself or in the person."

Mr. Lewes, in the "Westminster Review," * sums up the question concerning alcohol as a stimulant, as follows:—

---

* Westminster Review, No. cxxv., July, 1855, American edition pp. 59, 60. See also the Intellectual Development of Europe, p. 577, by Prof. John W. Draper, concerning the use of *food* by animals, for the *force* it contains. Also the able paper by Dr. Edward Smith, On the Actions of Alcohols, printed with the Transactions of the National Association for the Promotion of Social Science. London, 1860.

" Life is only possible under incessant stimulus. Organic processes depend on incessant change, and this change is dependent on stimuli. The stimulus of food, the stimulus of fresh air, the stimulus of exercise, are called natural, beneficial; the stimulus of alcohol seems selected for special reprobation without cause being shown, except that people choose to say it is not natural. How not natural? The phrase can have two significations, and it can have but two : first, that alcohol is not a stimulus which man employs in a state of nature; second, it is not consonant with the nature of his organism. The second is a pure begging of the question; and the first is in flat contradiction with experience. * * * No nation known to us has ever passed into the inventive condition of even rudimentary civilization without discovering, and, having discovered, without largely indulging in, the stimulus of alcohol. Man discovers fermentation as he discovers the tea-plant and the coffee-plant.

" Of two things, one ; either we must condemn *all* stimulus, and alcohol, because it is a stimulus ; or we must prove that there is something peculiar in the alcoholic stimulus which demarcates it from all others. Here, again, the reader sees the question narrowed and brought within an arena of precise debate. Only two positions are possible ; indeed, we may say, only one ; for who is mad enough to condemn all stimulus ? The ground thus cleared, the fight narrowed to this one point, let us do justice to the strength of our antagonist ; let us confess at once that there *is* a peculiarity in alcohol which justifies in some degree its bad reputation, a peculiarity upon which all the mischief of intoxication depends ; one which causes all the miseries so feelingly laid to its door. And what is this peculiarity ? Nothing less than the fascination of its virtue, the potency of its effect ; were it less alluring, it would not lure to excess; were it less potent, it would not leap into such flames of fiery exaltation."

Prof. J. F. W. Johnson, in his Chemistry of Common Life,* one of the most useful works of that distinguished chemist, says:—

"It is ascertained of ardent spirits, First. That they directly warm the body, and, by the changes they undergo in the blood, supply a portion of that carbonic acid and watery vapor which, as a necessity of life, are constantly being given off by the lungs. They so far, therefore, supply the place of food—of the fat and starch for example—which we usually eat. Hence a schnapps, in Germany, with a slice of lean dried meat, make a mixture like that of the starch and gluten in our bread, which is capable of feeding the body. So we either add sugar to milk, or take spirits along with it, (old man's milk,) for the purpose of adjusting the proportions of the ingredients more suitably to the constitution, or to the circumstances in which it is to be consumed.

"Second. That they diminish the absolute amount of matter usually given off by the lungs and the kidneys. They thus lessen, as tea and coffee do, the natural waste of the fat and tissues, and they necessarily diminish in an equal degree the quantity of ordinary food which is necessary to keep up the weight of the body. In other words, they have the property of making a given weight of food go further in sustaining the strength and bulk of the body. And, in addition to the saving of material thus effected, they ease and

* Vol. i., p. 349.

lighten the labor of the digestive organs, which, when the stomach is weak, is often a most valuable result.

"Hence fermented liquors, if otherwise suitable to the constitution, exercise a beneficial influence upon old people, and other weakly persons whose fat and tissues have begun to waste. * * * This lessening in weight or substance is one of the most usual consequences of the approach of old age. It is a common symptom of the decline of life. * * * Weak alcoholic drinks arrest or retard, and thus diminish the daily amount of this loss of substance. * * * Hence poets have called wine ' the milk of the old,' and scientific philosophy owns the propriety of the term. If it does not nourish the old so directly as milk nourishes the young, yet it certainly does aid in supporting and filling up their failing frames. And it is one of the happy consequences of a temperate youth and manhood, that this spirituous milk does not fail in its good effects when the weight of years begins to press upon us."

And now, with especial reference to alcohol both as food and as stimulus, the latest, and certainly one of the ablest, scientific authorities, is the recent work on "Stimulants and Narcotics" by Dr. Francis E. Anstie, lecturer on Materia Medica and Therapeutics, and formerly on Toxicology, at Westminster.

Dr. Anstie says:—

"If anything deserves the name of a *food*, assuredly oxygen does, for it is the most necessary element in every process of life. It is highly suggestive, then, to find that

that very same quiet and perfect action of the vital functions, without undue waste, without hurry, without pain, without *excessive* material growth, is precisely what we produce, when we produce any useful effect, by the *administration of stimulants*, though, as might be expected, our artificial means are weak and uncertain in their operation, compared with the great natural stimulus of life." (p. 145.)

" A stimulus promotes or restores some natural action, and is no more liable to be followed by *morbid* depression than is the revivifying influence of food. And if it be sought to distinguish foods by the peculiar characteristic of being *transformed in the body*, then I answer that this is the worst definition of food that can be given, since water, which is not transformed in the body at all, is nevertheless, the most necessary element of nutrition, seeing that human life cannot only not be maintained without it, but may subsist *for weeks* on water as its only pabulum besides the atmosphere and tissues." (p. 149.)

" Alcohol taken alone or with the addition alone of small quantities of water, will prolong life greatly beyond the period at which it must cease if no nourishment or water only had been given ; that in acute diseases it has repeatedly supported not only life, but even the bulk of the body during many days of abstinence from common foods ; and that, in a few instances persons have supported themselves almost solely on alcohol and inconsiderable quantities of water *for years*."

" We may be at a loss to explain the *chemistry* of its action on the body, but we may safely say that it acts as a food." (p. 138.)

" Another grand argument against the propriety of comparing stimulants with true foods has always been that *stimulus is invariably followed by reaction.* * * * It is *not true* that stimulus is of itself provocative of subsequent depression ; but there are circumstances in which this might easily appear to be the case. For instance, when the super-abundant mental energy of a man whose physical frame is weak, induces him to make violent and continued physical efforts, he is apt to find, at the end of a short ' spurt' of exertion, that his energy is exhausted. But here the exhaustion is no recoil from a state of stimulation. * * * And the case of drunkenness, that is, of alcoholic narcotism— affords another excellent example of the fallacy we are considering. The *narcotic* dose of alcohol, * * * is alone responsible for the symptoms of depressive reaction. Had a merely stimulant dose been administered, no depression would have occurred, any more than depression results from such a gentle stimulus of the muscular system as is implied in a healthy man taking a walk of three or four miles. What depression is there, as an after consequence, of a glass or two of wine taken at dinner, or of a glass of beer taken at lunch, by a healthy man ? What reaction from a tea-spoonful of sal-volatile swallowed by a person who feels somewhat faint ? What recoil from the stimulus of heat, applied in a hot bath, or of oxygen administered by Marshall Hall's process, to a half-drowned man ? *Absolutely none whatever."* (pp. 146–7.)

Doctor Brinton* says in his Treatise on Food and Digestion:—

" From good wine, in moderate quantities, there is no reaction whatever. * * * That teetotalism is com-

* *Treatise on Food and Digestion*, by William Brinton, M. D., F. R. S., Physician to St. Thomas' Hospital. (English.)

4

patible with health, it needs no elaborate facts to establish; but if we take the customary life of those constituting the masses of our inhabitants of towns, we shall find reason to wait before we assume that this result will extend to our population at large. And, in respect to experience, it is singular how few healthy teetotallers are to be met with in our ordinary inhabitants of cities. Glancing back over the many years during which this question has been forced upon the author by his professional duties, he may estimate that he has sedulously examined not less than 50,000 to 70,000 persons, including many thousands in perfect health. Wishing, and even expecting to find it otherwise, he is obliged to confess that he has hitherto met with but very few perfectly healthy middle-aged persons, successfully pursuing any arduous metropolitan calling under teetotal habits. On the other hand, he has known many total abstainers, whose apparently sound constitutions have given way with unusual and frightful rapidity when attacked by a casual sickness."

The emphasis of this opinion will be more fully appreciated, if one will but examine Dr. Brinton's book "On Diseases of the Stomach," which exhibits him in a most cautious and conservative light, in the remedial prescription of alcoholic drinks.

I come now very briefly to consider certain recent experiments upon which the prohibitionists mainly rely, to control the scientific opinions to which I have already alluded. I mean those of MM. Lallemand, Perrin, and Duroy. These ingenious French chemists, after a series of original experiments, supposed themselves to have proved that "*alcohol is eliminated from the organism in totality and in nature,*" and that it "*is never transformed, never destroyed in the organism.*" Their conclusion therefore, is, that "*alcohol is not food,*" as a scientific proposition, although as matter of practice they do go for light wines. In a pamphlet entitled "Is Alcohol Food or Physic," which I bought at the rooms of the "Temperance Alliance" in Boston, in which these gentlemen are upheld as supposed destroyers of the theory of which Liebig may be termed the father, I find that their experiments are contrasted favorably with others, because they were made on an empty stomach; and that these French experiments are confessedly pathological, rather than dietetic. The argument drawn from them, assumes, in great part, that inferences can be fairly drawn from effects produced by narcotic, or poisonous doses, (as for instance, the case of a man who died thirty-two hours after drinking a pint of brandy,) to the case of a person, using with temperance as a part of his meal, and in due proportion with other food, an article of mild drink in which it is combined. The same reasoning would in like manner, justify the argument that, because a decoction of green tea, of a given strength, will surely cause death, therefore a cup of weak tea taken with supper,—containing as it does, a portion of *theine*, the characteristic principle of tea,—is a deleterious drink, and proportionally poisonous. It also overlooks the mysterious subtleties of animal life, and those, still more mysterious and elusive, which connect the moral with the animal economy. It fails to observe the existence of a vital chemistry, some of the phenomena of which are observable, but whose laws thus far defy our capacity for logical definition. It even overlooks the varying action of the different alcoholic drinks, disclosed in the experiments of Dr. Edward Smith; for example, brandy and gin lessening the quantity of carbonic acid evolved in respiration, while it was increased, on the other hand, by the use of ale, and by the use of rum.

Animal chemistry is in its infancy. The positive knowledge on the points undertaken to be so dogmatically affirmed, on the strength of those recent French experiments, is relatively little; and men of science do not concur with their deductions.

Dr. Anstie, after having discussed and examined the many experiments both of Smith and of Lallemand and his friends, nevertheless declares, in view of their facts and those disclosed by the experiments of himself and of Baudot and others, his non-concurrence with the Lallemand theory; and, (comparing it with æther and chloroform,) he says of alcohol that it seems as if it " was intended to be the medicine of those ailments which are engendered of the *necessary* every day evils of civilized life, and has therefore been made attractive to the senses, and easily retained in the tissues, and in various ways approving itself to our judgment as *a food;* while the others, which are more rarely needed for their stimulant properties, and are chiefly valuable for their beneficent temporary poisonous action, by the help of which painful operations are sustained with impunity, are in a great measure deprived of these attractions, and of their facilities for entering and remaining in the system." *

One of the most able English scientific critics of these French experiments further says :†

" Dr. Brinton, [in his work on Food and Digestion,] who is by no means unreasonably prejudiced in favor of alcohol, has given it as the result of his very large experience, that persons who abstain altogether from alcohol, break down, almost invariably, after a certain number of years, if they

* Stimulants and Narcotics. p. 401.

† Cornhill Magazine, No. 33, September, 1862. Art., Does Alcohol act as a Food? p. 329.

are constantly employed in any severe intellectual or physical labor. Either their minds or their bodies give way suddenly, and the mischief once done is very hard to repair. This is quite in accordance with what I have myself observed, and with what I can gather from other medical men : and it speaks volumes concerning the way in which we ought to regard alcohol. If, indeed, it be a fact, that in a certain high state of civilization men require to take alcohol every day, in some shape or other, under penalty of breaking down prematurely in their work, it is idle to appeal to a set of imperfect chemical or physiological experiments, and to decide, on their evidence, that we ought to call alcohol a medicine or a poison, but not a food. In the name of common sense, why should we retain these ridiculous distinctions for any other purpose than to avoid catastrophes ? If it be well understood that a glass of good wine will relieve a man's depression and fatigue sufficiently to enable him to digest his dinner, and that a pint of gin taken at once will probably kill him stone dead, why haggle about words ? On the part of the medical profession, I think I may say that we have long since begun to believe that those medicines which really do benefit our patients act in one way or another as foods, and that some of the most decidedly poisonous substances are those which offer, in the form of small doses, the strongest example of a true food action ?

"On the part of alcohol, then, I venture to claim that though we all acknowledge it to be a poison, if taken during health in any but quite restricted doses, it is also a most valuable medicine-food. I am obliged to declare that the chemical evidence is as yet insufficient to give any complete explanation of its exact manner of action upon the system ; but that the practical facts are as striking as they could well

be, and that there can be no mistake about them. And I
have thought it proper that, while highly-colored statements
of the results of the new French researches are being somewhat disingenuously placed before the lay public, there
should not be a total silence on the part of those members
of the profession who do not see themselves called upon to
yield to the mere force of agitation."

And just a dozen years ago, Dr. James Jackson,
the venerable, beloved and most eminent Nestor
of the medical profession in America, bore this
public testimony concerning the medicinal employment of spirits and wines:—

"I would never order them to one whom I suspected to
be deficient in prudence and self-control. But, keeping
these things in mind, I have often directed the use even of
brandy. In doing this, I have been in the habit of saying
to the patient, 'If I ever hear of your indulging to excess
in the use of this, or any similar article, I will call on you
and exhort you to stop.' In one instance, and only one in
the course of a long life, have I been called upon to redeem
my pledge. This was in the case of a worthy lady, some
twenty years after I had directed the measured use of
brandy. At my request, she immediately gave up the use
of all spirituous and fermented liquors, and I have reason
to believe that she never resumed them. I do not, then,
call the risk very great of such prescriptions, when made
with proper caution. In regard to the benefit, in some
cases of dyspepsia, and in various other cases, I have not
any doubt. And, that I may tell the whole, let me say, that

I have repeatedly seen very great benefit from giving wine to young children. The benefit has been particularly marked in some children struggling feebly through the period of dentition, and I can name some to whom I had made this prescription more than forty years ago, among whom not one has shown any peculiar fondness for wine in subsequent years. I exhort all young people in health not to adopt the practice of drinking wine. I deprecate everything which shall tend to intemperance, and I believe that many men suffer from the use of wine and spirits, even in a moderate way. But I love to tell the truth, even when it is unfashionable. I believe that very many persons are benefited by the juice of the grape, and I choose to say so. Moreover, I believe that persons disposed to intemperance are not to be restrained from indulging their vicious propensity, by the abstinence of their more prudent neighbors." *

Professor Gairdner, of Edinburgh—while wholly opposing the theory of retarding the metamorphosis of tissue as a desirable end, and while admitting that to the perfect ideal man, living in the enjoyment of all natural and wholesome vital stimuli, amid perfect hygienic conditions, such liquors are probably worse than superfluous—declares his desire to leave all the physiological abstractions,

* Letters to a Young Physician just entering upon Practice, by Dr. James Jackson, M. D., LL.D., Professor Emeritus of the Theory and Practice of Physic in the University of Cambridge, late Physician Massachusetts General Hospital, Honorary Member of the Medico-Chirurgical Society of London, Corresponding Member of the Academy of Medicine at Paris, &c., &c., &c.

and to take his stand on the great broad series of recognized facts, which prove their relieving, reviving and supporting power under difficulties and in emergencies; claiming the right of reason to discriminate between their use and abuse. In that spirit he quotes in his work on " Clinical Medicine " this paragraph, from the " Letters to a Young Physician," calling it " *the whole matter in a nutshell.*"

Not content with my own unlearned reflections, nor even to leave the matter with Dr. Anstie, I called the subject as it is presented by Lallemand, to the attention of Dr. James C. White, the learned assistant-professor of chemistry in Harvard College. The report made by that gentleman, confirms the belief, in which Anstie had also concurred, that some alcohol is eliminated unchanged through the channels indicated by Lallemand and his friends; thus establishing an error in the previously held theory that, with the exception of a small amount which escaped by the lungs during expiration, this substance was *entirely* consumed within the organism. But he affirms that these experiments in no way prove that alcohol is eliminated *in totality* from the system; for the experiments on which that conclusion is based, furnish the strongest possible evidence of its unwarrantableness. The very experi-

5

ments on which alone they rest the conclusion that all which is taken into the animal economy escapes again unchanged, fail to discover any but a very small percentage discharged through the various channels of elimination. Yet the assertion is, that *all* has been thus eliminated; while if anything is proved at all, it is proved that alcohol is nearly all consumed within the organism, and that a very small percentage escapes unchanged. But it should be remembered that an excessive quantity of either salt or sugar being taken into the system, the excess is disposed of in the same way.

Of the proposition that "alcohol is never transformed, never destroyed" in the organism, Dr. White reports thus:—

"Former investigators had come to the conclusion that alcohol was converted into aldehyde and acetic acid, progressive products of oxygenation of alcohol, which in turn underwent further transformation, and that it finally escaped as carbonic acid and water. Lallemand, &c., examined the blood, after the use of alcohol, and failed to find either aldehyde or acetic acid, and on this negative evidence alone is based the sweeping conclusion. Even if we admit the correctness and fairness of their results which were obtained by experiments performed at too early a period to be completely satisfactory, and which are met by those of Bouchardet, *they in no way invalidate the theory of the transformation of alcohol in the organism.* We know too little of the many and complex changes which organic substances undergo within the economy, to speak in such positive terms. Those conclusions may or may not be adopted as to the conversion of alcohol into aldehyde and acetic acid ; *they certainly in no way settle the question as to its transformation or destruction in the system.*"

But, besides these proofs, you have in evidence before you the testimony of Dr. White in person, of Dr. Edward H. Clarke, Professor of Materia Medica, of Dr. Oliver Wendell Holmes, Professor of Anatomy and Physiology, of Dr. Henry J. Bigelow, Professor of Surgery, of Dr. J. B. S. Jackson, Professor of Morbid Anatomy and Pathology, and of Dr. D. Humphreys Storer, Professor of Obstetrics, (all in the Medical School of Harvard College;) of Dr. Charles T. Jackson and Professor E. N. Horsford, both eminent in chemistry and other branches of natural science. Those gentlemen constitute an array of experts in the sciences of chemistry, physiology and medicine, who are recognized as authority in the other hemisphere, as well as in our own. With their testimony before the Committee, forming a part of the printed record of its investigations, I need only allude to it without recital. I hold, that the opinions of these gentlemen, aided also by that of Pro-

fessor Agassiz, who testified to the *fact* of the use
of wine, with manifestly happy effects, in the actual
alimentation of European peoples, have for all the
purposes of legislative inquiry *established the dietetic uses of alcoholic beverages, when employed in
moderation, and properly combined in the construc-
tion of diet.* Their opinions again are re-inforced
by the recent physiological experiments tried with
ingenious variety in his own person, by Dr. Hammond, lately surgeon-general of the army of the
United States, and the conclusions arrived at by
that eminent physiologist.*

It does not follow, that because an old man, or
an ill-fed man, or an overtasked man, or an invalid,
may find alcoholic beverages useful, they are not
useless or hurtful to others. It does not follow,
that because they are good for some at sometimes,
they are good for all or at all times. Nor, on the
other hand, does it follow, because in their excess
and misapplication, they are indescribably bad, that,
"with bell, book and candle," they should be
solemnly cursed by the General Court.

This review of *the assumption that, because
alcohol taken in excess is injurious, it is therefore*

* See Hammond's "Physiological Memoirs," Philadelphia, 1863.

always a poison, will be soon ended. The statement of the proposition would seem to exhibit its fallacy, for it is arguing from abuse to use, and it is denying that difference in quantity can produce difference in quality.

The assertion is that, because alcohol taken into the system in certain quantities acts as a poison, it is therefore in all quantities and dilutions a poison. Let us examine it in the light of familiar illustrations. Omitting for the moment facts in evidence pertaining to alcohol itself, we have analogy perfect and to the point, in atmospheric air.

Atmospheric air is composed of, by weight, 23.01 of oxygen, and 76.99 of nitrogen. Each of the constituents of the air is essential to the present order of things. Oxygen is pre-eminently its *active* element. Duly to restrain this activity the oxygen is *diluted* and *weakened* by three times its bulk of the negative element—nitrogen. Their properties are thus *perfectly adjusted* to the requirements of the living world. Were the atmosphere wholly composed of nitrogen, life could never have been possible; were it to consist wholly of oxygen, other conditions remaining as they are, the world would run through its career with fearful rapidity; combustion, once excited, would proceed with ungovernable violence; animals would live with hundred-fold intensity, and perish in a few hours.

To infer from the effects of a large quantity to those of a less, is thus contrary to sound observation. *Oxygen*, pure, is a poison,—that is, we should die in it. Dilute it with three-fourths of nitrogen, and it becomes the air we breathe and by which all life is supported.

Saltpetre kills a man in doses of one ounce or upward. Eight ounces dissolved in a pint of water killed a horse. Two or three drachms only, will kill a dog. Nay, this very nitre or saltpetre may easily be a *remediless* poison.

" In acute rheumatism it is sometimes administered in doses repeated at intervals to the extent of two ounces in twenty-four hours ; though one-half ounce in concentrated solution causes heat and pain in the stomach which may be followed with convulsions and death. When taken in poisonous quantities there is *no antidote known.*"*

Yet, saltpetre is used without fear of evil consequences in the curing of hams and other meats. Shall we say that a sandwich is poisonous and should be prohibited by law?

* New American Cyclopœdia, Vol. xii., p. 377. Art. Nitre.

With one more quotation from the able pen of Mr. Lewes, I dismiss this fallacy from further argument:—

"When people say ' Oh, this is only a question. of degree,' they forget how frequently questions of *degree* involve questions of *kind*. Ice and steam differ only in the degree of heat; the cold of the Arctics and the heat of the Tropics are but differences of degree.

"Iron in a mass exposed to the air, burns, but burns so slowly that we call it *rust;* the same iron in a state of extreme subdivision *ignites* when exposed to the air. Here we have only differences of degree, yet if an inflammable substance be near the ignited powder, it will also ignite, whereas the same substance might remain forever close by the rusting iron and never be affected. If this be true in cases so simple, how much more should we expect to find it in cases so complex as those of organic processes where minute variations ramify into vast and unforeseen results!

"The argument from excess is worthless. It only meets cases of excess. Oxygen is as terrible a poison as strychnine, if in excess. Heat, so indispensable to the organism, is obliged to be reduced to moderate quantities before the organism can endure it. Light, which is the necessary stimulus to the eye, produces blindness, in excess; mutton-chops have, when taken in moderation, a nutritive value which no Briton is bold enough to question, * * * yet mutton-chops taken in excess kill with the certainty of arsenic, for *over-*nutrition is fatal."

And now, in concluding my remarks upon what I have termed the scientific view of the question, I repeat, in the words of Mr. Lewes:—

" Let no advocate of temperance misconstrue the present [argument.] We rescue a scientific question, we do not oppose the moral principles of the movement. That drunkenness is one of the most terrible sources of demoralization, and that temperance, both physically and morally, is one of the cardinal virtues most needing inculcation, no reasonable being doubts. Equally indisputable is it that any movement which can effect a reform in the tendency to drunkenness, deserves the heartiest support. Nor are we surprised at the exaggerations and errors which such a movement employs as instruments to effect its purpose. * * * Our purpose, then, be it understood, is not to cast a stone of obstruction in the path of the temperance movement, but to argue a scientific question."

This much, at all events, is clear, viz.: *That the Legislature of Massachusetts has no knowledge, and has no means of knowing, that the classification, (so commonly and so authoritatively made,) by which alcohol, as found in certain drinks, is included in the category of foods, is not correct.* If that classification *is* correct, then there is an end of the

controversy. For then it cannot be held that the
government ought to prohibit the citizen from
making up his own bill of fare for himself; though
he can be held accountable for his evil conduct
affecting others, proceeding from his abusing this
liberty. But those who insist on the existing
statute of prohibition, in spite of the fact that those
drinks are foods, or that they may be such, and
that most masters of chemistry and physiology
have so taught, and that the successive gener-
ations of men have so believed, and that the
most venerable exemplars of all human history
have confirmed that belief by their own examples,
and that a great portion of the people of Massachusetts think so now, and at least demand the
right of deciding the question for themselves,—
those who thus insist, dare to propose to drive
rough-shod over all respect for the convictions of
their neighbors, and, assuming a theory entirely
modern, (and at the best, uncertain and contro-
verted,) to continue and to enforce the pains and
the disgraces of the criminal law in its support.
*If the proposition, on which alone prohibition by
the government can possibly stand, is true, let it be
proved.* I, certainly, for one, having meditated
upon it, and observed upon it for years, have not

seen it established. I am entirely willing to find it true. And if it is true, I desire that its truth shall be made clear. But I want it established by methods fit to be pursued by free and rational men. I desire that every obstacle may be removed from the path of inquiry, and that the minds of all the people may be disabused of every just ground of prejudice, and be made hospitable and receptive. I know that wilfulness and violence, even under the forms of law, can only arouse contradiction and resentment. I know that, besides these, there will continue to be aroused an honest sense of personal injustice inflicted by the operation of statutes believed to be founded on incorrect notions, arbitrarily insisted upon, and obstinately adhered to. While such relations last, there is no opportunity for men on either side to reach the best conclusions. The mere war of words is of itself always sufficiently disturbing. But, it seems an almost wanton disregard of the laws and the rights of the human mind, to complicate and distract, as the upholders of this law have done, the moral and intellectual issues which the whole subject involves. Grant that you have much reason to believe the proposition of the Prohibitionists true, I submit that no honest man can yet declare that it is proved.

Nay—outside of the lists of controversy—where are the intelligent judges who are prepared to affirm that it enjoys even the *preponderance* of the proofs?

I honor these scholars, whose testimony has been cited, for their ingenious pursuit of science. I should never fear that such men would draw extreme conclusions, nor insist on their premature adoption by others; for learning is modest.

That alcohol can be easily fatal; that it is hurtful always,—unless taken both in moderation, and under circumstances, and in compounds, and in combinations, adapted to the physical condition and the true needs of the individual,—there is no possible dispute. But that all the drinks into which it enters, are to be of course dietetically rejected, is not, thus far, the verdict. Nor does it yet appear that any experiments have settled the boundaries within which diet shall be kept. A physician once starved to death a duck, by feeding it solely on butter. It lived three weeks, and until the butter oozed through its skin and dropped from its feathers.* Yet butter is not a poison. We know very well that a man could not maintain

* Boussingault,—Chimie Agricole, p. 166; quoted in Treatise on Physiology, by Prof. John C. Dalton, p. 108.

health, nor even life, long, on water to drink and sugar to eat. Yet neither is a *poison*. Dr. Stark actually died in the experiment of trying to live on cheese. Yet everybody knows that cheese is a rich and nutritious food. The instances might be indefinitely multiplied of proofs in our common observation, of the inability of single articles of acknowledged wholesome and nutritious solid food to maintain life and health, used singly and without variety. For example, how long would a man live in Havana, on pork only? How long would a healthy Greenlander subsist, amid his snows, on oranges? Or, how long could we, in Boston even, live on either? The common experience of men certainly goes for something. Now the common experience of many nations and ages having assigned a place in the foods and medicines, to stimulating drinks of some kinds, into which alcohol enters—the experiments of chemists and physiologists are pursued, when made in the interest of truth and pure science, with a view to detecting, identifying and comparing their modes of operation, and correcting the errors of inadvertence in common life. And when the men of science have come to any substantial agreement, which calls on the civil state to interpose and alter the practice of society, in order to conform it to the decrees of science, we shall learn it from the men of science themselves; we shall not be called on by the unlearned to settle such disputes of the learned by an Act of the Legislature.

Within my own memory Dr. Sylvester Graham taught that no permanent cure for intemperance could be found, except in such changes of personal and social customs as would relieve the human being of all desire for stimulants. He soon applied the idea to medicine, so that the prevention and cure of disease, as well as the remedy for intemperance, were found by him in the resort of all mankind, without regard to age, climate or condition, to the use of water as the only beverage, and the eating of vegetables to the entire exclusion of animal food. And I confess that he seemed to prove it. His theories were ingenious, fortified by elaborate argument. They would have been very good, save that almost all the rest of mankind saw that they were not true. Even some of the very experiments on which he relied, contradict his too rash and dogmatical generalization.

> " A little learning is a dangerous thing:
> Drink *deep*, or taste not the Pierian spring."

Had Graham convinced many, as for a time he did convince a few, then we might to-day have been arguing as a question of legislative prohibition, the case of Rhine wines and porter in company with that of mutton chops and beef steaks, all being included in the like condemnation.

II.

Leaving here, gentlemen, the argument on the assumption by the Prohibitionists that *alcoholic beverages are essentially poisonous*, I pass to the argument on their further assumption, that *the use and the sale of alcoholic beverages are essentially immoral.*

The evils of this world are too great to render exaggeration any more consistent with wisdom than with truth. What we need is courage, not cowardice, for the controversy against them. This world is a trying one to live in at all. But when its discipline is complete we shall go hence. After all, the moral dangers are within ourselves, not in the objects of nature. And social evils find their causes mainly in the falseness and disorder of the social economy. The savage ignorantly ascribes malign purposes and supernatural powers to things

sometimes the most inanimate and senseless. He
sees them in some near relation, real or fancied, to
woes already endured or evils apprehended. He
seeks to conciliate them by worship. And that we
justly call *superstition*. But civilized man is not
wholly unlike him. Sometimes, perceiving that in
human society, in affairs, even in the uses of natural
things, and in the operation of the passions native
to the very constitution of the race, there are mani-
fold abuses, he flees, disheartened and disgusted,
from human society, abjures affairs, despises nature
and all her loveliness, and contradicts and quarrels
with all the intimations of nature within himself.

It is only in the strife and actual controversy of
life—natural, human and free—that robust virtue
can be attained, or positive good accomplished. It
is only in similar freedom alike from bondage and
pupilage, alike from the prohibitions of artificial
legislation on the one hand, and superstitious fears
on the other, that nations or peoples can become
thrifty, happy and great. Will you venture to
adhere to the effete blunders of antiquated despot-
isms, in the hope of serving, by legal force, the
moral welfare of your posterity ? Will you insist
on the dogma that, even if certain gifts of nature
or science are not poisons, they are nevertheless so

dangerously seductive that no virtue can be trusted to resist them ? But when society shall have intrusted the keeping of its virtue to the criminal laws, who will guaranty *your* success in the experiment, tried by so many nations and ages, resulting always in failure and defeat ? Do you exclaim, that the permitted sale of these beverages, followed as it must be by some use, must be followed, in turn, by some drunkenness; and that drunkenness is not only the parent cause of nearly all our social woes, but that it is impossible to maintain against its ravages a successful moral war ? To both these propositions, moral philosophy, human experience, and history, all command a respectful dissent.

Reason, experience and history all unite to prove that, while drunkenness lies in near relations with poverty and other miseries, and is very often their proximate cause, it is not true that it is the parent, or essential cause, without which they would not have been. And to the teachings of reason, experience and history, are added the promises of Gospel Grace, enabling me in all boldness, to confront the fears of those who would rest the hopes of humanity on the commandments of men.

The evils of society, in our own country and in the northern nations, have always tended to appear on the surface in the form of this sensual indulgence. And yet, the essential evil has always been less deeply seated, while at the same time, the hope of social regeneration is brighter, within them, than among some other peoples, in whom the instinctive love of liberty is weaker, and among whom such indulgence is comparatively unknown.

Writing in 1799, Croker says in his " Travels in Spain ":—

" The habitual temperance of these people is really astonishing; *I never saw a Spaniard drink a second glass of wine.* With the lower order of people, a piece of bread with an apple, an onion, or a pomegranate, is their usual repast."

And many writers and travellers at different periods concur in describing them as temperate, frugal, and even abstemious as a rule, testifying that " drunkenness is a vice almost unknown in Spain among people of a respectable class, and even very uncommon among the lower orders."

An English clergyman, eight years ago, in 1859, describing a tour through Spain, remarks, that when they were approaching the plains of Castile:—

7

" It had now become quite evident, from the number of beggars, male and female, adult and juvenile, with their tattered brown clothing and mahogany complexion, that we were at length in veritable Spain." *

Again he says :†—

" In all our wanderings through town and country, along the highways and by-ways of the land, from Bayonne to Gibraltar, we never saw more than four men who were in the least intoxicated. If they would only leave off those two national sins, bad language and misuse of the knife, they would be some of the finest peasantry in the world."

Our own distinguished fellow-citizen, William Cullen Bryant, in a series of letters written in 1857, says :—

" The only narcotic in which the Spaniards indulge to any extent is tobacco, in favor of which I have nothing to say ; yet it should be remembered in extenuation, that they are tempted to this habit by the want of something else to do ; that they husband their cigarritos by smoking with great deliberation, making a little tobacco go a great way, and that they dilute its narcotic fumes with those of the paper in which it is folded. *With regard to the use of wine, I can confirm all that has been said of Spanish sobriety and moderation.*"

But Spain, though once prosperous and rich, became in spite of the temperance and abstinence

* Roberts's Autumn Tour in Spain," p. 61.   † pp. 320, 321.

of her people, miserably and frightfully poor. Her manufactures, once the means of employment of hundreds of thousands of workmen, passed into decay and neglect. Her agriculture at the beginning of the present century failed to supply wheat enough for the consumption of her people. And notwithstanding many institutions of hospitality and charity, maintained by the ecclesiastical orders, and by contributions from the public funds, the poor are so numerous, that beggary in some of the provinces is considered no disgrace, and even students have been known to occupy their vacations in excursions to raise by begging, the means required for their personal support, labor being regarded by them as more disreputable than asking alms. Supremely ignorant, notwithstanding the acknowledged gravity, sobriety, sincerity and generosity of the Spanish character, the people are miserably poor in the midst of fertility of almost tropical exuberance. And their country,—possessing within herself nearly every mineral and vegetable production needful or convenient to mankind, holding numerous ports, and a geographical position commanding greater commercial advantages than any other country in Europe, but without the idea of liberty,—sleeps, a torpid mass, a giant prostrate and powerless, bound by the principles and traditions of five hundred years ago. Notwithstanding the abstinence of her people from the indulgence of the bowl, neither her future nor her present would offer any temptations to the people of New England.

Do not let us deceive ourselves into reversing the order of our own history. If drunkenness is the essential parent cause, and not usually the mere concomitant or consequence, of social degradation, there ought to be a time found somewhere far back in the former ages, when our own ancestors were sober, virtuous and happy; but when, visited by the seductive fruit of the vine, and falling into the snare of unwonted and alluring temptation, the shadow of a great woe came over them, never to pass away until the wine shall cease to redden in the cup. But the truth is otherwise. There has never been any such day of innocence and happiness, since Adam was banished from Eden. And yet, it is not difficult to trace back the steps of the progress of that country from which most Americans sprung, to times long before the introduction of spirits, or wines, or beer, or even ale itself into England.

The Britons, prior to the Roman conquest, knew so little of agriculture, were so rude and barbarous, that the strongest liquor they had, was *mead*, or honey mixed with water and allowed to ferment,— a product of the rudest and simplest kind, and of which the quantity possible must have been of necessity very little. But nevertheless, those were days of the spiritual domination of the Druids, of the darkest superstition, and of the brutal sacrifice of innocent human victims.

Under the Anglo-Saxons, parents are known to have exposed their children in the market place for sale like cattle. The poverty of the poor and the helplessness of their lot were such that on occasions of famine, to which in former times, England, rich, fertile and merry, but ignorant and unthrifty, was no stranger, many of them who were free, having no means of living, sold themselves into slavery. During all the feudal ages, private wars raged constantly. The feudal lords lived in a state of war against each other, and of rapine towards all mankind. A great portion of the people were helpless bondmen. All Europe was a scene of internal anarchy during the middle ages, and though England was less exposed to the scourge of private war than most nations on the conti-

nent, she endured tumultuous rapine and frightful
social disorder. The whole population of England, covering a territory seven or eight times as
large as Massachusetts, was not, five hundred years
ago, a million greater in number than the present
inhabitants of our own Commonwealth. When
Latin ceased to be a living language, the newly
formed, or modern tongues, not being used in public documents or correspondence, the very use of
books or letters was almost wholly unknown to
the people. Schools, confined to cathedrals and
monasteries, and exclusively designed for ecclesiastical purposes, afforded no encouragement or
opportunity to the laity. It was rare for one of
them, of whatever rank, to be able to write his
name. Even the minor clergy were sometimes
unable to translate into their own language the
words they chanted in the celebration of the mass.
The barons tyrannized over both serfs and tenants,
and from the oppression of their absolute will the
humble and despised could expect little redress and
no permanent relief. The rudeness of agriculture,
the absence of enterprising, intelligent commerce,
the utter poverty of science, the discouragement of
all the arts by the nobles who scorned everything
but arms, kept down the poor, and rendered the

masses both hopeless and contemptible. War, slavery and ignorance could not fail to exhibit as their natural concomitant, the coarse, sensual indulgence of appetite, both excessive and depraved. Revelry and wassail distinguished the festivities and rejoicings of victory and the celebration of public events, invaded the solemnities of the church, and divided with indolence and the chase the empire of private life, whenever arms were silent. And what better fate or fortune could have been expected for the common poor, the serf, the follower, the retainer, than the humble and remote imitation of his lord?

The people were saved from the sense of insupportable misery, of conscious degradation, and of infinite hopelessness, by the brutishness of manners and their capacity for low enjoyments. Humanity, like Psyche in Grecian fable, enduring servitude and trial, wandering about in search of her lost but immortal love, is invisibly comforted and sustained. She wears always the wings which will one day unfold themselves for flight, when, purified both by passion and misfortune, she is ready for happiness in re-union with the lover whose immortality she has come to share. Wandering, like the maiden from temple to temple, scorned, buffeted and oppressed, humanity retreats behind mortality, which shelters while it beclouds the soul. A tender and divine spirit is forever watching over her, softening calamity, whispering hope, providing deliverance, and assisting her conquest. By a universal law of nature, matter gravitates. But by a universal spiritual law, the soul aspires. There is a limit to moral disease. There is always a balm, and a physician in Gilead. The cure is often slow; but the patient lives forever.

Descending to a later era, I need only to borrow Macaulay's vivid picture of the character of England during the century between the Tudors and the Guelphs:

"There is scarcely a page of the history or lighter literature of the seventeenth century which does not contain some proof that our ancestors were less humane than their posterity. The discipline of workshops, of schools, of private families, though not more efficient than at present, were infinitely harsher. Masters, well born and bred, were in the habit of beating their servants. Pedagogues knew no way of imparting knowledge but by beating their pupils. Husbands, of decent station, were not ashamed to beat their wives. The implacability of hostile factions was such as we can scarcely conceive. Whigs were disposed to murmur because Stafford was suffered to die without seeing his bowels burned before his face. Tories reviled and insulted Russell as his coach passed from the Tower to the scaffold in Lincoln's Inn

Fields. As little mercy was shown by the populace to suf-
ferers of a humbler rank. If an offender was put into the
pillory, it was well if he escaped with life from the shower
of brick-bats and paving-stones. If he was tied to the cart's
tail, the crowd pressed round him, imploring the hangman
to give it the fellow well, and make him howl. Gentlemen
arranged parties of pleasure to Bridewell on court days, for the
purpose of seeing the wretched women who beat hemp there
whipped. A man pressed to death for refusing to plead, a
woman burned for coining, excited less sympany than is
now felt for a galled horse or an over-driven ox. Fights,
compared with which a boxing-match is a refined and humane
spectacle, were among the favorite diversions of a large part
of the town. Multitudes assembled to see gladiators hack
each other to pieces with deadly weapons, and shouted with
delight when one of the combatants lost a finger or an eye.
The prisons were hells on earth, seminaries of every crime,
and of every disease. At the assizes, the lean and yellow
culprits brought with them from their cells to the dock an
atmosphere of stench and pestilence which sometimes avenged
them signally on bench, bar, and jury. But on all this misery society looked with profound indifference. Nowhere
could be found that sensitive and restless compassion which
has, in our time, extended a powerful protection to the fac-
tory child, to the Hindoo widow, to the negro slave, which
peers into the stores and water-casks of every emigrant ship,
which winces at every lash laid on the back of a drunken
soldier, which will not suffer the thief in the hulks to be ill-
fed or over-worked, and which has repeatedly endeavored to
save the life even of the murderer." *

* Macaulay's History of England, Vol. i., pp. 394, 395, (Harper's octavo
edition.)

A hundred years ago, in the habits of the best Englishmen, there existed the traces and consequences of the old demoralization. England was free. The long agony with the Stuarts was over. A new era had begun, of fame, of prosperity, of culture, of opportunity for the people, of literature, of ideas. But the social disease was not cured. The best were still afflicted by it. Drunkenness still remained, as one of its symptoms and expressions, on the upper surface and in the purest society. Bigotry, both religious and political, was a repulsive and characteristic feature of the country gentleman. He hated his neighbor, of different opinions, because they differed. The machinery of both Whig and Tory was unlimited bribery. The "Folly" coffee-house was his resort in town, where rural ladies listened to words of compliment from the wits and beaux of the time, which those of our own time would not dare to read. The duchess and the courtesan were alike visitors, where the gay maskers indulged in the allusions and jests of a corrupt taste and a licensed opportunity. " At the beginning of the eighteenth century," (says a recent historian,) " and long after, we see no struggle against great social evils, on the part of the clergy or the laity. Every attempt at social reform was left to the legislature, which was utterly indifferent to those manifestations of wickedness and crime, that ought to have been dealt with by the strong hand. Education, in any large sense, there was none. Disease pursued its ravages, unchecked by any attempt to mitigate the evils of standing pools before the cottage door, and pestilent ditches in the towns. * * * There were evils so abhorrent to humanity, that their endurance, without the slightest endeavor to mitigate or remove them, was an opprobrium of that age. The horrible state of the prisons was well known. The nosegay laid on the desk of the judge at every assize proclaimed that starvation and filth were sweeping away far more than perished by the executioner, terrible as that number was. * * * London, and all other great towns, were swarming with destitute children, who slept in ash-holes, and at street doors. They were left to starve, and in due course to become thieves, and be hanged. * * *One-fifth of the whole population were paupers."*

Disease, filth, ignorance, licentious manners, neglect of human want and woe, judicial cruelty, and pauperism! It needs only *drunkenness* to complete the picture. *It was not the cause of all*

* Popular History of England, by Charles Knight, Vol. v., page 60.

this. But it was a necessary concomitant; a part of the natural expression of an almost infinite inward evil. And I sometimes wonder whether, in permitting so many to yield to this merely sensual indulgence of *brutish men,* Divine Providence had not saved them from becoming *human devils.* That feature was not wanting, in the age to which I allude. I will allow the same historian to finish the description.

Quoting from the " Guardian," he goes on to say: "' A method of spending one's time agreeably is a thing so little studied, that the common amusement of our young gentlemen, especially of such as are at a distance from those of the first breeding, is drinking.' Yet we have abundant evidence that those ' of the first breeding' were often the most intemperate. The *moralists* were not exempt from the common vice of our *young gentlemen.* Swift says: ' I dined with Mr. Addison and Dick Stuart, Lord Mountjoy's brother, a treat of Addison's. They were half *fuddled,* but not I, for I mixed water with my wine.' "

Gaming was the universal passion of the reign of Anne. In the first number of the " Tatler," it is said of Will's Coffee House: " This place is very much altered since Mr. Dryden frequented it.

Where you used to see songs, epigrams and satires, in the hands of every one you met, you have now only a pack of cards. Into these places of public resort the lowest sharpers found their way; and gentlemen were not ashamed to stake their money against the money of the most infamous of society."

In Italy, writes Steele, " a cobbler may be heard working to an opera tune; and there is not a laborer or handicraftman that, in the cool of the evening, does not relieve himself with solos and sonnets." But, " on the contrary, our honest countrymen have so little inclination to music, that they seldom begin to sing until they are *drunk*." Sir John Hawkins has described the musical entertainments which were offered to the middle classes at this period. He says that "the landlords of public houses hired performers, and hither came very unrefined audiences, to *drink* and to smoke."

Writing of English life and manners, at about the end of the last century, or just after the American Revolution, Miss Martineau thus exhibits the same connection of sensual vulgarity on the surface, with deep and pervading contempt of the sacredness of humanity at the core:—*

* History of England, from 1816 to 1854, with an Introduction, 1800 to 1815.   Vol. i., p. 28, 29.

" While the course of daily living was hard to the working man, and his future precarious, the Law was very cruel. The records of the Assizes in the Chronicle of Events are sickening to read. The vast and absurd variety of offences for which men and women were sentenced to death by the score, out of which one-third or so were really hanged, gives now an impression of devilish levity in dealing with human life; and must, at the time, have precluded all rational conception on the part of the many, as to what Law is, to say nothing of that attachment to it, and reverence and trust in regard to it, which are indispensable to the true citizen temper."

" The general health was at a lower average among all these distresses than was even safe for a people who might at any moment have to struggle for their existence. *The habit of intemperance in wine was still prevalent among gentlemen*, so that we read of one public man after another whose death or incapacity was ascribable to disease from *drinking*. Members of the cabinet, members of parliament and others, are quietly reported to have said this and that *when they were drunk*. The spirit decanters were brought out in the evenings in middle-class houses, as a matter of course; and gout and other liver and stomach disorders were prevalent to a degree which the children of our time have no conception of. During the scarcity, the diseases of scarcity abounded, of course."

But allow me in a moment to relieve the picture. You all know how mighty and universal has been the movement of the nineteenth century. The axe has been laid at the root of the tree. There has

been a patient, hopeful, scientific and learned, as
well as a pious, philanthropy. The disease was
a radical disease. The cure is a *radical reform.*
The recognition of the people, of their wants and
woes, their essential capacity, their rights, their
progressive tendency, their citizenship, their humanity, the oneness of man with his brother man,
the benignant fatherhood of Almighty God,—this
recognition, which exposes the littleness of worldly
distinction in the presence of this unity of the
brotherhood, has waked up the intelligence, the
heart and soul of England, to the work of studious
and persistent reform, as radical as the malady of
which Love is the healer and Justice the medicine.

Dating back from the middle to the beginning
of this nineteenth century, what had been accomplished in this work ? The vice of drunkenness
had gradually disappeared, with the coarseness, of
which it was the natural expression, giving way to
those humanizing and refining influences, with
which sensual and brutal manners are inconsis-
tent.

"One of the most distinguished of Frenchmen
comes as ambassador to England in 1840, and
regarding with a philosophical intelligence both the
great and the humble, he thus contrasts the past

with the present. Looking back to the end of the eighteenth century, he says that there were at that time, even in the elevated classes of English society, many remains of gross and disorderly manners. Precisely because England had been for centuries a country of liberty, the most opposite results of that liberty had been developed in startling contrasts. A puritan severity was maintained side by side with the corruptions of the courts of Charles II. and the first Georges; habits almost barbarous kept their hold in the midst of the progress of civilization; the splendor of power and of riches had not banished from the higher social regions the excesses of a vulgar intemperance. Even the elevation of ideas and the supremacy of talent did not always carry with them delicacy of taste; for the Sheridan who had been electrifying parliament by his eloquence might the same night have been picked up drunk in the streets."

"M. Guizot goes on to say, 'It is in our time that these shocking incongruities in the state of manners in England have vanished, and that English society has become as polished as it is free; where gross habits are constrained to be hidden or to be reformed, and where civilization is day by day showing itself more general and more harmonious.'

Two conditions of progress, he continues, which rarely go together, have been developed and attained during half a century in England. The laws of morality have been strengthened, and manners have at the same time become softer, less inclined to violent excesses, more elegant." *

This eminent French writer and statesman says also that the double progress of a stricter morality, and a refinement of manners, was not confined to the higher and middle classes, but was very apparent amongst the bulk of the people. " The domestic life, laborious and regular, extends its empire over these classes. *They comprehend, they seek, they enjoy, more honest and more delicate pleasures than brutal quarrels or drunkenness.* The amelioration is certainly very incomplete. Gross passions and disorderly habits are always fermenting in the bosom of obscure and idle misery; and in London, Manchester, or Glasgow, there are ample materials for the most hideous descriptions. But take it all in all, civilization and liberty have in England, during the course of the nineteenth century, turned to the profit of good rather than of evil. Religious faith, Christian charity, philanthropic benevolence, the

* Popular History of England, by Charles Knight, Vol. viii., pp. 401, 402.

9

intelligent and indefatigable activity of the higher classes, and good sense spread amongst all classes, have battled, and now battle effectually against the vices of society, and the evil inclinations of human nature." *

This progress was not mechanical. It was dynamic. It was not Jewish, nor Mohammedan; but it was Christian. It was not due to law, but to liberty. It came not from the thunders of burning Sinai, but from the silent inward voice.

A writer in the " Democratic Review," in 1848, discussing the topic of " Poverty and Misery " in their relation to " Reform and Progress," mainly in the direction of politics, laments the apparent defeat of the people in the successive popular struggles of the old world. He records the continued existence of the old poverty and misery, with modifications only, notwithstanding the promise which heralded the revolutions of that period. He turns from cause to cause, from the nostrum of one political doctor to the palmistry of another, and slides at last into an exclamation of despair at the experience of the old world, and the prospect at home, in view of the unknown cause of what he discovered at last

---

* Guizot—" Mémoires pour servir à l'histoire de mon temps," Tome v., 1862.

was " *a general and obstinate disease.*" "From statistics lately published," he remarks, when alluding to France, "it appears that one-eighth of her population are habitually clothed in rags; that nearly three-fifths never eat wheaten bread; that very nearly two-thirds wear wooden clogs instead of shoes; * * * and more than ten-elevenths of the whole population cannot afford to consume sugar and animal food." How much of this continued depression and poverty was to be ascribed to drinking the wines of France may be seen in the fact that a more efficient prohibition was found in the very poverty of the masses than ever slumbered in the arm of legislative power. For " *more than three-fourths* " of the whole population were shown by the same statistics, and declared by the same writer, in the same sentence, to be so poor that " *they cannot get wine to drink,*" notwithstanding that is and was a staple of the country. The truth, I think, may be discovered by looking straight down to the bottom of the well. The French people inherited the consequences logically flowing from earlier barbarism, from Roman conquests, from tribal, local, private and national wars, from the feudal servitudes, partly seen in a debt mortgaging the lands of the people, and weighing them down by an

annual interest exceeding that of the public debt
of Great Britain, leaving the proprietors and cultivators not more than twenty-four per cent. of the
whole annual production, for the maintenance of
their families, while the low estate of agriculture,
(which means again the absence of science and
machinery,) gave an average yield of only fourteen
bushels of wheat, or twenty bushels of potatoes, to
an acre of ground.

Thirty years ago, at the accession of Victoria,
the public mind had been already somewhat aroused
by the report of a distinguished architect, concerning a district in London in which dwelt squalid misery, in perishing houses, undrained, unventilated,
in pestilential alleys, where the typhus and every
form of epidemic and contagion always rioted.
Soon after, inquiries promoted by parliament were
extended through formal commissions into other
large cities of England and Wales, and into Scotland. Mr. Chadwick's report* exhibits the frightful
result of a death-rate among these poor unfortu-
nates of the lowest classes, doubling the mortality
of their opulent neighbors. This mortality was
largely owing to habits of filth and intemperance,

* Report of the Poor Law Commission.

but those habits were induced by the unavoidable degradation of physical causes which no virtue could override. "In closed courts where the sunshine never penetrated; where a breath of fresh air never circulated; where noxious vapors filled every corner from the horrible cesspools; where the density of population was so excessive, as in itself to be sufficient to produce disease; where a single room was often occupied by a whole family, without regard to age or sex,—the wonder is how the poor lived at all, uncared for by the rich who knew them not, neglected by their employers, who, in some trades exposed them to labor in workshops not far superior in ventilation to the Black Hole of Calcutta. Amongst these careless and avaricious employers, the master tailors were the most notorious, who would huddle sixty or eighty workmen close together, nearly knee to knee, in a room fifty feet long by twenty feet broad, lighted from above, where the temperature in summer was thirty degrees higher than the temperature outside. Young men from the country fainted when they were first confined in such a life-destroying prison: the maturer ones *sustained themselves by gin*, till they perished of consumption, or typhus, or delirium tremens."*

* Popular History of England, by Charles Knight, Vol. viii., p. 392.

One of the most eminent of living physiologists says, "Mr. Chadwick has shown that many are *driven to drinking gin as affording a temporary relief* to the feelings of depression and exhaustion produced by living in a noxious atmosphere." *

Sir James Tennent, seven years ago, addressing the institution for promoting Social Science, speaks of the condition of the Irish laborers in England, of whom much complaint had been made for their habits of tippling and pauperism. So late as 1860, he describes them as in the possession of "unwholesome dwellings in the most unhealthy portions" of the great cities, in whose "comfortless apartments domestic enjoyment is little known and the inmates are inured from infancy to miasma, damp and decay." "Their food," he says, was "in quality, of the poorest by which existence can be maintained," and they enjoyed "*the single excitement of intoxication.*"

The testimony of the patient and philosophical Liebig is given, with the emphasis of positive opinion. "In many places destitution and misery have been ascribed to the increasing use of spirits. This is an error. *The use of spirits is not the cause, but an effect, of poverty.* It is an exception

---

* Psychological Inquiries, by Sir Benjamin C. Brodie, p. 78.

from the rule when a well-fed man becomes a spirit drinker. On the other hand, when the laborer earns by his work less than is required to provide the amount of food which is indispensable in order to restore fully his working powers, an unyielding, inexorable law or necessity compels him to have recourse to spirits. He must work, but in consequence of insufficient food, a certain portion of his working power is daily wanting. Spirits, by their action on the nerves, enable him to make up the deficient power at the expense of his body; to consume to-day that quantity which ought naturally to have been employed a day later. He draws, so to speak, a bill on his health, which must always be renewed, because, for want of means he cannot take up; he consumes his capital instead of his interest; and the result is the inevitable bankruptcy of his body."*

Bad as the condition is of the laboring classes in England, Mr. McCulloch, the political economist, writing in 1854, affirms that the condition of most classes of work-people had improved since the close of the American war; that they were better fed, better clothed and better lodged, than at any former period. "Drunkenness and immorality,"

* Letters on Chemistry, 3d London edition, p. 455.

he adds, "if they have not materially abated, have not increased; while the manners of all classes have been humanized and softened." He affirms also, that "great improvement had taken place in the health and in the longevity of the population." Admitting that "the condition of the laboring class is far from prosperous," and that "the middle classes have always evinced far more prudence and forethought than those below them," he testifies that the work-people of the present day are less vicious and improvident, and more industrious, than their predecessors of any former age. But, why have not the humblest laboring class, while accomplishing their own measure of progress, equalled their superiors of the middle class in the ratio of advancement? It is simply because—as a wise writer says—"wretchedness is incompatible with excellence: you can never make a wise and virtuous people out of a starving one."

Nor can more be demanded of a body of men, on whom has accumulated the weight of centuries of wrong. For the great mass of the English poor is nothing but the continuation of the race of villeins or slaves, whose servitude to the baron has been exchanged for dependence on the parish and subordination to the powers of society scarcely less degrading. The emancipated serf had lived a life of thoughtless and hopeless dependence, without instructed prudence or trained forethought, in the midst of those who contemned his weakness and his low estate. In times of pervading ignorance, and when society was too unskilled and unthrifty to protect itself against constantly recurring famine, he had received the form of personal freedom, but not its power. And thus the vices and sensuality of a thousand years, and the essential evil out of which they grew, descending and reappearing in some variety but substantial identity, age by age, linger longest and will die out the latest in that class of men rendered comparatively worthless by servitude.

But even *they* have illustrated the recuperative energy of human nature,—the power of moral agencies and awakened intelligence to renew and restore. I cannot but give honor to the social reformers, preaching the truths of nature and her science, for the deliverance of the suffering poor, and I give honor also to that very class of weary and depressed laborers, for their response. The degradation of circumstances has yielded already. Theirs never was a voluntary depravity which elected drunkenness for the mere love of gin, and accepted misery for the sake of the bowl. As social science advances, as society itself leads, so they will continue to follow. They may yet be brutish, yea, and drunken too; but *drunkenness will disappear as the light shines in on the darkened intellect, as opportunity develops manhood, as hope visits and encourages the heart.*

Crime and tippling are so linked together, that if we could banish tippling, the judges have a thousand times declared that crime, unable to live alone, would follow too. But crime is already going. The influences of which I speak have already diminished crime, by striking at the common causes of crime and drunkenness both. The population of England and Wales in 1849, is given in the " Statesman's Year Book " at 17,552,000, and in 1863, (or fourteen years later,) at 20,554,137—an increase of a little more than three millions. But the number of convictions for crime in the same period descended from 21,001 to 15,799,—a diminution of criminal offenders of 5,202, or a little less than twenty-five per cent. In other words, while in 1849 the number of criminal offenders was in the proportion of one in 835 of the aggregate population, in 1863 the fraction had fallen to one in 1,300. The average number of children attending school had more than doubled. Similar, though less striking results, appear in Scotland. And in Ireland, the apparent diminution of criminal offence is so remarkable and unprecedented, that while something must perhaps be allowed to improvement in police and judicial organization, I am confident that the social history of the island is a still more brilliant example of the powerful moral effect produced by the material and educational advancement of a people.

Less than three years ago, John Bright, the great political and social reformer, in a speech opposing in the House of Commons a bill for more restrictive treatment of the sale of alcoholic beverages, bears his own testimony to the progress made in those classes most accessible to moral influence and the motive of ideas:—

" I am old enough to remember, when among those classes with which we are more familiar than with the working people, drunkenness was ten or twenty times more common than it is at present. I have been in this House twenty years, and during that time I have often partaken of the hospitality of various members of the House, and I must confess that during the whole of those twenty years, I have no recollection of having seen one single person, at any gentleman's table, who has been in the condition which would be at all fairly described by saying that he was drunk. And

I may say more,—that I do not recollect more than two or three occasions, during that time, in which I have observed * * * that any gentleman had taken so much as to impair his judgment.

"That is not the state of things which prevailed in this country fifty or sixty years ago. We know, therefore, as respects this class of persons,—who can always obtain as much of these pernicious articles as they desire to have, because price to them is no object,—that temperance has made great way; and if it were possible now to make all classes in this country as temperate as those of whom I have just spoken, we should be amongst the very soberest nations of the earth."

If I am asked to account for the disappearance of drunkenness among the more favored classes, I appeal to the same cause which has purified literature, ameliorated the criminal code, banished torture and religious persecution, wrought out "Catholic emancipation," extended the ballot, established "model houses" and "ragged schools," encouraged innocent amusements, cultivated music and the arts, dismissed the barbarity of duelling, descended with Howard and Elizabeth Fry into the prisons, has flown with Florence Nightingale to the battle-field, and penetrated the various abodes where "lonely want retires to die," into all the wretched retreats of misery, and all the dungeons where society exacts the penalty of crime.

I appeal to the same universal spirit and the same unerring law which renders it "more blessed to give than to receive." Intelligence, a higher, purer, more liberal culture, wider views and more knowledge, and all the material and scientific, as well as moral characteristics of modern civilization have combined to make the Ehglishman more "brave, tender and true;" therefore more a *gentleman* of self-respect and refined manners, as well as a man more reverent of the divine image seen in all our common human nature. Could Plantaganets, Tudors and Stuarts, wielding despotic powers; could the sovereign pontiff fulminating the professed decrees of heaven, and denouncing the terrors of hell; could all their powers combined, their earthly penalties and eternal pains, have accomplished this moral regeneration? No, gentlemen, you know they could not have done it. As the Apostle taught of the Early Church, so true philosophy declares of the secular corporation of human society; that *we are one body and members one of another.* The same God who revealed something more than was yet known of the laws of the natural universe to one, taught cunning inventions in mechanism to another, spread out the broad pages and unfolded the sealed books of human history to another, and uncovered to another the mysteries of this throbbing heart and this scheming brain, has in like manner inspired others with loftier ideas of Right, and anointed their eyes with clearer visions of Duty. All these have become leaders of the people, and co-operators in the great social regeneration.

The same phenomena have been manifested on our own side of the Atlantic. Like causes here have in like manner purified, softened, refined the habits of social life at home. And the excesses of gluttony and drunkenness which used to mar the festivities of former times have, so far as I have ever been a witness, and as the proof shows, disappeared. But there has never been on earth any human *governmental* power which could have brought it to pass. The *law* possesses absolutely no reforming power. It can punish, can terrify, hold in forcible restraint. It cannot convert nor can it touch the springs of feeling or of thought. Unconvinced, untouched, unconverted, do you suppose the ingenuity and the armies of the world could have devised a statute and concentrated a force which could have dominated personal habits in those spheres of society, and have made any permanent and pervading impression on social conduct and private manners?

Drunkenness was naturally one of the forms which vice assumed in New England. So far as it depended on the mere fact of opportunity for indulgence, it was partly due to our nearness to the West Indies, and to the trade by which our lumber was exchanged for their molasses. The peculiar product of our distillation was the result of the lumber trade with the West India Islands, just as the production of whiskey is now the result of the superabundant grain crops of the Western States. A hard climate, much exposure, little variety in food, and great want of culinary skill, few amusements, the absence of light cheering beverages, a sense of care and responsibility cultivated intensely, and the prevalence of ascetic and gloomy theories of life, duty and Providence— have, in time past, all combined to increase the perils of the people from the seductive narcotic. A man whose virtue was weak, or whose discouragements were great, or whose burdens were heavy, or in whom the spirit waged unequal war with the allurements of the flesh; or even one in whom a certain native gayety strove with the unwelcome exactions of the elders, was often easily its victim. Independence, intelligence, self-respect, broader views, kinder and tenderer sympathies, the cultivation of the finer tastes, the love and appreciation of beauty, a truer humanity—not to speak of better social theories—all made more general and pervading in our society—have gradually by divine favor been made instrumental in the deliverance of our people from that bondage. I have not mentioned *a greater conscientiousness* in the catalogue of causes, for I do not believe that conscientiousness has ever been greater than in New England, nor that it is greater now than it was in other times. It was a characteristic of New England from the first. It was always a source of greatness in her people. But it has been often morbid and even superstitious.

The evil of drunkenness needed to be met by a gracious Gospel kindling the heart, not by a crushing sense of guilt goading the conscience. The temperance reformation sprung up out of the heart of a deeply moved humanity. It was truly and genuinely a Gospel work. It was a mission of love and hope. And the power with which it wrought was the evidence of its inspiration. While it held fast by its original simplicity, while it pleaded, with the self-forgetfulness of Gospel discipleship, and sought out with the generosity of an all-embracing charity, while it twined itself around the heart-strings and quietly persuaded the erring, or with an honest boldness rebuked without anger,—it was strong in the Lord and in the power of his might, verifying the prophecy of old, that one might chase a thousand and two put ten thousand to flight. But when it passed out of the hands of its Evangelists and passed into the hands of the centurions and the hirelings; when it became a part of the capital of political speculation, and went into the jugglery of the caucus; when men voted to lay abstinence as a burden on their neighbors, while they felt no duty of such abstinence themselves, (even under the laws of their own creation); when the Gospel, the Christian Church and the ministers of religion were yoked to the car of a political triumph; then it became the victim of one of the most ancient and most dangerous of all the delusions of history.

Mr. Frederick Hill, an English barrister, and formerly "Inspector of Prisons," in a work published in London in 1853, discussed in a spirit of intelligent philanthropy the topic of "Crime: its Amount, Causes and Remedies." He declares his belief, " as the result of many years of inquiry and observation," that crime "is steadily decreasing and

11

taking a milder and milder form;" and that this decrease is not only positive but comparative; so that notwithstanding the increased wealth and population, " and estimating the extent of crime by the average amount of privation, fear and suffering which it causes to each member of society, the decrease is great indeed."

He classifies the "chief causes" of crime thus: "1. Bad training and ignorance. 2. Drunkenness and other kinds of profligacy. 3. Poverty. 4. Habits of violating the laws, engendered by the creation of artificial offences. 5. Other measures of legislation interfering unnecessarily in private actions or presenting examples of injustice. 6. Temptations to crime caused by the probability of escape or subjection to insufficient punishment."

Two of these are very suggestive. *Artificial Offences*, and *Meddlesome Legislation*, and that felt to be unjust, are indeed causes of crime of which the philosophical legislator cannot afford to be ignorant. Artificial offences put a large class of people, and often that the least discriminating and instructed, into needless antagonism with the law. Confounding of moral distinctions on the side of the law, begets a corresponding confusion in the mind of the citizen. If the law treats the sale of

a mug of beer, or sweet cider, as of like delin-
quency with the crime of larceny, how long will it
take the humble and the unlearned to conclude that
the law is either a sham, unworthy of veneration,
or else to jump to the converse of the first proposition, and vote the larceny of an article to be no
worse than the selling of the beer or the cider?
So, therefore, every statute denouncing the penalties of the criminal law against men, in violation
of the commonly received sense of justice concerning human relations in the civil state, becomes,
by reason of that very excess, a generator of evil.
The laws under which men are punishable, can
have no moral value unless the appeal can also be
made to the consciences of men; challenging them
boldly to the confession of the apostle, "Where-
fore the law is holy, and the commandment holy,
and just, and good."

But, I pray your attention now to the first three
in the category of causes of crime: *Ignorance
and bad training—Drunkenness and other kinds of
profligacy—Poverty*. And when you shall have
seen, (what all investigation proves,) how few ever
fall into the criminal class, who have had the advantages of the simplest elements of learning—the
acquisition of the power to read and write well

their own tongue; who have even been taught any trade involving skill; and who have enjoyed immunity from the miseries of poverty; you then will see how drunkenness itself yields to motive and encouragement.

Against the common notion that the poorer classes commit fewer penal offences when they are straitened by seasons of unusual poverty, than they do when they are not so poor as to be unable to get drink, Mr. Hill opposes the result of his wide observation as Inspector of Prisons. Against this opinion Mr. Hill sets " *the general fact that, in periods of prosperity, our* [*their*] *prisons are comparatively empty.*" The truth was undoubtedly just this—and it is undoubtedly true here as in England—*the ignorant, neglected, poverty-stricken and forlorn are also drunken.*

But, do you urge that if you can maintain your statute of prohibition, you will remove the temptation of drunkenness out of their way—gaining thus much, at least; and that, besides, you will gain a better chance to attack ignorance and poverty with success? I reply that if men were simply intelligent machines there might be something in your plan. The error in your plan is that you allow nothing for the human will, nothing for the elasticity and enterprise with which it accommodates itself to new exigencies, whenever you challenge a direct combat between the law on the one hand and the purpose of even the humblest of the people on the other hand. The denunciations of positive law, unsustained by a successful appeal to the prevailing sense of right and justice, are little else than a trumpet-call to battle. Let the effort be the prohibition of a dangerous but seductive beverage, and let the period be a dark age, or let the manners of the time be generally gross and coarse, or let the amusements of the people be few and their intelligence low, or let there be a class of underfed and dejected laborers, or beggars—and the effect will be as disastrous as the experience of England in 1737, of Sweden long ago, and of Scotland. Both McCulloch in his book on " Taxation," and Porter in his " Progress of the Nation," have portrayed the failure of the English experiment. The reaction was both swift and irresistible.

In the " charges " of Recorder Hill of Birmingham, whose long and earnest devotion to the removal of drunkenness entitles him to universal gratitude, we find a discussion of English prohibition. He affirms that " the impediments thrown in the way of the venders of alcoholic drinks, partly by the imposition of duties on the manufacture or importation of the article, and partly by the system of licenses, had diminished, or at all events kept in check the consumption of intoxicating liquors. We need, gentlemen, no statistics to prove to us, that the state of the country in 1830, was much better in regard to temperance than it was a century before that period." But the philanthropic Recorder utters one sentence in describing the fate of the legislation of 1737, [which was the same statute alluded to in the testimony of Mr. Derby,] which (coming from a judge, in whose heart both the idea of liberty, and the sentiment of humanity had alike a share,) is an emphatic admonition to ourselves. It is in these very words: *"And doubtless it could only have been successful among a people, who to the sensuality and ignorance of the English populace should have added the slavish obedience of the Russian serf."*

In Sweden, notwithstanding the laws against intoxication, rigorously enforced, and those forbidding the gift or the sale of spirituous liquors to workmen, servants, soldiers, minors, &c., the distillation by the people in their own houses carried up the production of spirits to an annual average of ten gallons for each inhabitant. In Scotland, we are informed by the Temperance Prize-Essay of Doct. Lees, that in the second century, Argadus, the administrator of the realm, pulled down the houses of the sellers of strong drink, confiscated their goods and banished the men; that in the ninth century Constantine II. added· the punishment of death to the taverners who resisted the decree; that in the sixteenth century, although there were no public taverns known, the citizens brewed their own ale, "their usual drink," and *they* entertained the travellers; that in just one hundred years later, multitudes of drunken beggars infested Scotland, and in plentiful years, robbed poor people living remote from neighbors, and used to meet in the mountains feasting and rioting for days together, and that on all public occasions they were found, both men and women, "perpetually drunk." The sheriff of Lanarkshire, Mr. Allison, testified* in 1838, that at every tenth house in Glasgow spirits were sold, and that the whiskey drunk in Glasgow was probably twice or thrice as much as in any similar population on the globe.

The report by the Secretary of the Board of State Charities of Massachusetts, just printed (covering the year 1866,) declares in these emphatic

* Porter's Progress of the Nation, p. 679.

words: "*It is notorious that the great mass of criminals is made up of the poor, the ill-taught, the ill-conditioned, and, in a double sense, the unfortunate.*"

"The proportion in the Commonwealth of those who cannot read and write, among persons capable of crime, is between *six* and *seven* per cent., while the proportion of criminals who cannot read and write, for the last ten years, has been between *thirty* and *forty* per cent. *or more than five times as great.*"

"Out of 11,260 prisoners, only 429, *or less than one in twenty-five*, are reported as ever having owned the value of $1,000."

The Secretary mentions that 7,343, or about two-thirds of this number, are set down as intemperate, which he deems too low an estimate.

Those figures show that the social law I have so often affirmed, holds good in Massachusetts, and up to the present time. It is from "the poor, the ill-taught, the ill-conditioned, and in a double sense, the unfortunate," that the ranks of pauperism and insanity, and crime and drunkenness, are yearly reinforced. It is true that the Secretary speaks of drunkenness as the "chief occasion of crime." And that it is connected or associated with crime, being one of the symptoms of the same disease of which crime is another, one of the manifestations of social degradation, one of the proximate causes too of many an offence, is true. But—let me put a case which will illustrate the true relation of drinking to crime. A few years ago, a young man, not twenty years old, who had never been to school, nor to church, had never learned his letters, had never heard the blessed name of Jesus, save when profanely uttered, urged by the desire of his wife for money, and goaded by her taunts, loaded his gun with powder and shot, and loaded himself with whiskey and gunpowder, and marched forth to the highway, and shot to death another man, (then travelling his rounds to deliver, as it happened, liquors to his country customers,) and robbed him on the spot. At his trial nearly all the witnesses, being residents of the same neighborhood, unable to write their names, *made their mark* only, on the certificate-book of the officer. I suppose this murder is reckoned among the crimes chargeable to drinking. And, perhaps, the mixture of whiskey and gunpowder which he drank, blunted his nerves and calmed his agitation, and thus fortified his audacity, to the extent of enabling him to do what would otherwise have been too much for him. Without

12

such drink, perhaps, and without a gun, certainly, he would never have shot his victim. But the *purpose* of violence and robbery was formed before he drank. The crime was sufficiently complete, as a purpose of the mind, without the draught. What made him a felon in the purpose of his heart? What degraded him into an ignorant heathen, living in the midst of a society where the fashions and customs and desires of modern civilization serve to inflame the natural passions of those who are forbidden to share in its opposing influences of refinement and religion? If you should urge the prohibition of alcoholic drinks because of such an event, attributing the event to their having passed the lips of the felon—in one word, charging the murder to the whiskey—let me ask you what you would say about the thousand or thousands of the young men, who no doubt, drank on that same day, in the same county, and whose reputations are unspotted by offence? But—those young men, you will reply, did not drink to madness, or inebriation. Then, it was not the *use* of the draught, but its *abuse*—voluntary and wicked—which, logically, you ought to hold up to rebuke, and hold out as a warning. Nor is that all. There were many young men that very day, who drank when they ought to have abstained, who drank foolishly, dangerously, intemperately—but who otherwise committed no offence. Why were not they, too, felons, or at least peace-breakers? Why did *they* not even overstep the bounds of apparent, public decorum? Because they had culture, means of high enjoyment, were restrained by fine influences and social happiness; because they were not of "the poor, the ill-taught, the ill-conditioned, and in a double sense, the unfortunate."

When you charge crime to drunkenness, as one of the frequent proximate causes of crime; and when you charge the sinking of many a man into deeper degradation, by abandoning hope, and abandoning himself to drinking as one of the seductive forms of sensuality, you are right. But much that I hear, leads me to dread the return to our Christian community, of that pharisaic morality which substitutes a ritual conformity, in matters not essential in nature nor by the divine law, for the heart of love and the embrace of charity.

The report of the Secretary, in 1864, avows the belief "that no less than three-fourths of what is technically called crime among us, is the *direct* result of *poverty* and its attendant evils." A year later, alluding to that remark, he adds, "I did not mean to be understood that mere lack of money is a potent cause of crime. There is a poverty which is honorable and conducive to virtue, just as there is an affluence which tends to the growth of every vice. But that degree of poverty which excludes education, which abases and finally destroys self-respect, which breeds disease, indolence and vice, is conspicuous in every civilized country, and conspicuous as a curse. Of such did the wise man say, ' The *destruction* of the poor is their poverty.' "

M. Dupuy, the Director of the French prisons, in his report for 1863, exhibits a diagram showing that, for twenty years, crime against property in France has risen and fallen with the price of grain.

And it is a fact in remarkable confirmation of the theory of these gentlemen, that in our own Commonwealth, crime diminished not only during the years of the rebellion, but was less during the very last year, and has not at any-time risen to the amount of detected crime existing before the war. The number of women committed in 1866, was ten per cent. less, and the number of children twenty-five per cent. less, than in 1865. Not even the flow of bad whiskey with which, on the evidence, the whole country is suffering a deluge, has been able to counteract the moral advantages to the humbler classes gained from the pay, bounties, state aid and high wages of the last few years. There was a constant accumulation of savings, all over the Commonwealth, among persons in humble life, which is evidence of increased comfort, sure to produce greater hopefulness and self-respect.

Still does not poverty owe its own origin oftentimes to drunkenness? Undoubtedly, yes. So also is it due often to luxury and idleness originating in bad moral training, the sudden acquisition of unearned wealth, leading to habits of self-indulgence degenerating into drunkenness and other vices. But, drunkenness in our own modern society, ending in either pauperism or crime, in one of good training, grounded in reasonable intelligence, with the means of comfort, and supported by the inspirations of hope, is a rare and exceptional phenomenon. Drunkenness is, however, one of several causes immediately generating crime and pauperism—the reduction of which to the minimum, is one of the studies and aims of civilization. Yet, the effort to reduce them by a war on the *material* abused to produce drunkenness, is scarcely less philosophical, than would be an attempt to prevent idleness and luxury, by abolishing property and imitating the legislation of Sparta.

I aver that a statute of prohibition, aiming to banish from the table of an American citizen by pains and penalties, an article of diet, which a large body of the people believe to be legitimate, which the law does not even pretend to exclude from the category of commercial articles, which in every nation, and in some form in 'all history, has held its place among the necessities or the luxuries of society, is absurdly weak, or else it is fatal to any liberty. Whenever it will cease to be absurdly weak, society by the operation of moral causes, will have reached a point where it will have become useless; or else it will be fatal to any liberty, since, if not useless, but operated and fulfilled by legal force, its execution will be perpetrated upon a body of subjects in whose abject characters there will be combined the essential qualities which are needful to cowardice and servility.

Do you tell me, that no beverage into which alcohol enters, used in cooking, or placed upon the table, fitly belongs to the catalogue of foods?

I answer: *That is a question of science,* which neither governor nor legislature has any lawful capacity to solve for the people.

Do you tell me, then, that whether the catalogue be expurgated or not, all such food is unwholesome and unfit to be safely taken?

I answer: *That is a question of dietetics.* And it is for the profession of medicine. There is, in principle, no odds between *pro*scribing an article of diet and *pre*scribing a dose of physic, by authority of law. The next step will be to provide for the taking of calomel, antimony and Epsom salts by Act of the General Court.

Do you tell me, however, that all such beverages, in their most innocent use, involve a certain danger; that possibly any one *may*, probably many, and certainly some *will*, abuse it, and thus abuse themselves; and by consequence that all men, as matter of prudence, and therefore of duty, ought to abstain from and reject it.

I answer: *That is a question of morals,* for the answer to which we must resort to the Bible, or to the Church, or to the teachings of moral philosophy. The right to answer it at all, or to pretend to any opinion upon it, binding the citizen, has never been committed by the people, in any free government on earth, to the decision of the secular power. If the State can pass between the citizen and his Church, his Bible, his Conscience and God, upon questions of his own personal habits, and decide what he shall do, on merely moral grounds, then it has authority to invade the domain of thought, as well as of private life, and prescribe bounds to freedom of conscience. There is no barrier, in principle, where the government must stop, short of the establishment of a State Church, prescribed by law, and maintained by persecution.

Do you tell me that the using of wine or beer as a beverage, however temperately, is of dangerous tendency by reason of its example? Do you insist that the temperate use of it by one man may be pleaded by another as the occasion and apology for its abuse?

I answer: that if the government restrains the one man of his own just, rational liberty to regulate his private conduct and affairs, in matters innocent in themselves, wherein he offends not against peace, public decorum, good order, nor the personal rights of any, then the government both usurps undelegated powers, and assumes to punish one man in advance for the possible fault of another. The argument that, because one man may offend, another must be restrained, is the lowest foundation of tyranny, the corner-stone of despotism. Liberty is never denied to the people anywhere, on the ground that liberty is denied to be good or right, in itself. The universal pretext of every despotism is, that liberty is dangerous to society,—that is, that the people are unfit to enjoy it.

Do you tell me that these arguments have a tendency indirectly to encourage and defend useless and harmful drinking, and that silence would have been better—for the sake of a great and holy cause?

I answer: that He who governs the universe and created the nature of man, who made freedom a necessity of his development, and the capacity to choose between good and evil the crowning dignity of his reason, knew better than to trust it to the expedients of political society. The great and holy cause of emancipation from vice and moral bondage, is moral, and not political.

It used to be thought right to burn a man's body for the salvation of his soul. It used to be thought that to suppress heresy and false teachers deceiving the people, was mercy to the heretic and the false teacher themselves, while it protected the people against perversion and spiritual ruin. The motive was not bad, but the philosophy was fatal. The better the motive, the sincerer the men, the more

13

disastrous was the policy. So now, if *dishonest* and *despotic* men alone, from love of power and not of human welfare, should appeal to this machinery, to work, against men's wills, their moral renovation, the plan would lose more than half its danger. But the bad precedents *good* men establish to-day, in the weakness of their faith in better means, *bad* men use to-morrow for bad purposes and with worse motives. Meanwhile, aiming at compulsory conformity to your creed of artificial virtue, the dissentients, even if submissive, regarding themselves merely as the victims of a dominant asceticism, are made deaf to moral teachings, impatient of the preacher, haters of his doctrine, and defiant at heart.

Gentlemen, I maintain the positions I have assumed, and enforce them by arguments, because I believe those positions to be true, and the arguments sound. I believe it is safe, expedient and wise to stand by the truth. If the Catholic priest, uttering the united voice of all the bishops and minor clergy of the principal ecclesiastical body in Christendom, [see testimony of Rev. James A. Healey,] claims no power to declare that to be a sin, which Almighty God has not made to be a sin, neither can Protestant minister nor popular convention. But, I cannot stand in the attitude of *defence*. If the doctrine is true; if the teachings of science are so; if the argument is sound, then I charge back upon all those who, in the spirit of jesuitical philosophy would sacrifice the truth, science and argument, to a supposed moral expediency, *that they—in the service of morality—are unsettling its foundations in the confidence of men.*

Do you suppose that the adherents of the Roman Catholic Church, or the many thousands of other persuasions, whose opinions have been declared by the reverend and learned men, belonging to Protestant denominations, who have denied before this Committee the moral validity of the theory of prohibition, will accept the dogmas of a Protestant Pope, although indorsed by a self-created convention, or enacted by a secular government? Do you suppose that the people of every class and persuasion,—taught by professors and practitioners of medical science of every school to take wines and beer as tonics, and restoratives, and as part of their diet, in illness, in age, or on occasions of physical depression—will, in their hearts, believe your declaration that they are essentially and characteristically poisonous? Do you think that the children at our firesides will believe that the apostle, (in the unworthy phrase of modern discussion,) was a "rummy" and a perverter, when, instead of commanding total abstinence, he enjoined freedom from excess of wine? Do you imagine they will forget, that he who made the best wine which the guests enjoyed at the marriage feast in Galilee, (because He came "eating and drinking" while John the Baptist was a Nazarite and drank no wine,) was aspersed by the Jewish Pharisees as a "*wine bibber* and a friend of publicans and sinners"?

The people and the children are not blind to the inconsistencies and sophistries of those who claim to lead them. They can distinguish the truths of the Gospel, and the practical dictates of Reason, from the controversial theories of "contentious conscientiousness."

I have a few words to say on the statistics. Many gentlemen called by the remonstrants, gave opinions based on the presumed existence of facts which, if *not known* to exist, can afford no ground of opinion. If *known*, they could have been *proved*, by reference to the ordinary means of statistical information. For the purpose of aiding the Committee to arrive at the truth, we brought the evidence of such gentlemen to the test of cross-examination; in every instance showing that their opinions, whenever they seemed at first to have been deductions from such facts, were in reality, at best, only the *guesses* of honest, but pre-occupied judgments. Now there was one gentleman whose fame in statistics, in philanthropy and in medicine, had led to his employment by the national government to prepare the volume of "Mortality" in the series of volumes containing the results of the census of 1860—I mean Dr. Edward Jarvis. An ardent opponent of all "ardent spirits," he would have been for the remonstrants the safest possible witness, had the truth been trustworthy. He was the best witness for them to have called, had they only desired the best evidence. Besides, I had alluded to his work, in my cross-examinations. And on the last day of their testimony, one of the most intelligent and fair-minded of their witnesses, when pressed in cross-examination by the facts shown in the statistics of Dr. Jarvis's volume, repeatedly called in question the reliability of the census reports. The Doctor, (who knew better than anybody else,) was in the presence of the Committee during the larger part of the sitting. He had also been in the hall, with the witnesses, through the whole day on Wednesday, and several times before. I had early notified the remonstrants that I desired, should they call him to the stand, to have it done when present myself.

They used up Wednesday, and they used up Friday; (Thursday I was absent in court;) but Dr. Jarvis was kept silent, while very unimportant things were put in proof. At last, five minutes after the time of the sitting had been exhausted, and the chairman had declared an adjournment, Dr. Jarvis was called by Rev. Dr. Miner to the stand, and the special favor granted, of ten minutes for him to make a statement. He read some passages from the French treatise of M. Morel, on the " Dégénerescences de l'Espèce Humaine," about the evil effects—exhibited in sterility, impotence, insanity, idiotcy, and the like—of the " *abuse* " of alcohol, and what Morel scientifically terms, " chronic alcoholism,"—touching all which there is no dispute. He then produced and put into the case some tabular matter, *not read by us, nor to us;* when the necessity of clearing the hall for the sitting of the House itself, ended the testimony. *Nor was any opportunity possible for cross-examination.* I have no idea that *Dr. Jarvis* desires anything but the truth, of which he is an earnest, toilsome investigator, with an enthusiasm for a dry mass of figures, which he is always willing to trust, "hit where it will." The remonstrants had *seemed*, on the record, to have called Dr. Jarvis, and they had *seemed* to have got us into the position of voluntarily omitting to cross-examine. But what Dr. Jarvis had to say *as a statistician*, no one was enabled either to hear or to read. I made no complaint at the time. I knew that if I should object to the allowance of the ten minutes, it would seem ungracious to a venerable and learned man, and perhaps be otherwise misconceived. Besides, I thought then (and so I think now) that the remonstrants, by their stroke of apparent finesse, when fully understood, would only gain a loss.

When we depart from the simplicity of truth as it is found in nature, in the lives of the great exemplars of our race, and in revealed religion, and go to hewing out for ourselves the broken cisterns of merely human ingenuity, we are not unlikely to tend to run the experiment into palpable extremes, and to try it too often.

Let me add: in regard to Morel, it appears that his dissertation on "chronic alcoholism" is founded on observation of 200 cases, and that, of these, thirty-five were cases in which the ungovernable appetite for excess was caused *by disease*.*

Of the sheets handed in from Doctor Jarvis, I am obliged to confess that it has been impossible yet fully to explore their figures or even to decipher them. Yet two or three points may be discussed.

Among the reasons urged why Massachusetts should resort to methods which belong to "*military necessity*" rather than civil administration, is, in substance, though not in form, *the averment of the existence of such a necessity*. This is a convenient plea, often just, but sometimes abused, even in war ; never justifiable in peace and when no overwhelming and sudden exigency of convulsion, fire, flood, or pestilence returns society to its original rights, which organized government may, on those supreme occasions, be unable to vindicate under the forms of regular procedure. Among the proofs of such a *necessity* to transcend the sphere of legislation, break down the precedents, and disregard the principles of liberty, (as they have been understood by men of English blood, ever since the Revolution of 1688,) is the alleged fact of a desperate and frightful mass of *insanity*, existing in this country and occasioned by drink.

* Traité des Degénérescences, physiques, intellectuelles et morales de l'Espèce Humaine, par le Docteur B. A. Morel. Paris, 1857, p. 132.

Doctor Jarvis is an especial expert in the cure of insanity, as well as in the study of its phenomena, and its literature. On one of his sheets is a table " of patients admitted into hospitals for the insane, caused by intemperance." This table states that, of all the patients received into all the hospitals in the United States down to 1856, the causes of their disease as reported are known in 14,935 cases. The cause of the insanity of 1,536 is reported to have been " intemperance." That number is the aggregate of known alcoholic insanity, out of all the aggregate population existing during a series of years running from 1833 to 1856, and that too, making no allowance for recommittals of the same persons, who must in some instances be enumerated twice. It gives a gross ratio of 1,028 cases of " insanity caused by intemperance," out of each 10,000 reported cases. Now, let us compare this result with the figures given on the same page, showing the experience of the different hospitals and different sections of country relatively to each other. I do this for the purpose of learning whether in those parts of the country where prohibitory legislation prevails, any apparent diminution of this kind of insanity has arisen. Also, I do it to learn whether in those parts where liquors are plenty and cheap, this insanity is proportionally increased, by the tables.

14

Also, to test the accuracy of the *reasoning* of the physicians, the friends of patients and others, to whom we are indebted for the statements in the individual cases assigning the insanity of patients to this cause. I say the " *reasoning*," because, while I do not deny their truthfulness, I am not so sure of their accuracy in correctly discriminating between apparent causes and real ones, between causes immediate and causes remote.

Remember that the grand ratio in the Union, by these statistics, is 1,028 to 10,000—a trifle over one in ten. But, in Ohio, (whence came a witness for the remonstrants, to say how much his people longed for the legislation of Maine and Massachusetts, and New England generally, against the sale of alcoholics,) Dr. Jarvis's table shows only 505 out of 10,000, or a trifle less than one-half the average ratio of intemperate insanity in the country. Compare the State of Ohio with Massachusetts. The returns for Boston, Dr. Jarvis's table gives as showing 2,318 out of 10,000, or more than twice the average ratio of the Union; Northampton Hospital, 2,168, Taunton Hospital, 2,379, and Worcester Hospital vibrating at different periods from 1,110, up to 1,832. Go to Philadelphia, and the ratio found in the whole period returned is 1,183. The highest ratio there was from the years 1856 to 1866, when it was at the rate of 1,310 to the 10,000. The average ratio of all the Pennsylvania Hospitals is 1,064 to the 10,000; while Harrisburg Hospital presents a ratio of only 547 to the 10,000.

This table then proves, if it proves anything at all, that " insanity from intemperance," as it is returned, prevails more in the very head-quarters of prohibitory legislation and principles, than it does in the whiskey region of the West and the North-West, where, before the war-tax, whiskey could have been bought at the distilleries for a quarter of a dollar the gallon, and where also the manufacture of wine from the native grape has grown to be an important business of the people, and " prohibition " is known only by name.

I will admit, however, that *prohibition*, as such, may be excluded from the argument. It has really existed in New England, only *in name*. And, it is fair to give the remonstrants the benefit of the fact in the argument. But it is true, that a large degree of *abstinence*, even to totality, has existed in New England, *in fact*, ever since these hospital records began to be made. How shall we account then for the fact, which, the remonstrants have themselves thus proved, that Massachusetts, admitted to be so far ahead of Pennsylvania and Ohio, in technical or ritual temperance, suffers from twice to four times as much, from insanity caused by intemperance, as they do? I suppose the truth to be, that the real or primary cause of much of the insanity of men falling into intemperate habits, and reported as made crazy by those habits, could be traced to anterior causes. These, distracting, breaking down, weakening and disheartening the man, in mind and body, left him to topple over into drunkenness, in which condition he first disclosed occasion for anxiety to his friends, and from which, by the rapid development of the undiscerned, though earlier, malady, he descended rapidly into some form of positive, visible insanity, of which drunkenness, as the last antecedent, became the apparent cause. On this point I might content myself with merely citing the testimony of Dr. Morel himself in his very treatise * which was quoted by Dr. Jarvis on other points. By means of drinking, it became known, for the first time, that the patient was crazy at all. And, this

* Traité des Degénérescences, etc., by Dr. Morel, page 133, note; where the learned author says: "Les débuts de l'aliènatèon mentale offrent une telle complexité, qu'il est bien difficile aux parents de se fixer sur l'influence principale sous laquelle se développe le mal. Il arrive bien souvent que telle cause qu'ils regardent comme efficiente, n'est souvent qu'un effet secondaire."

"The beginnings of mental alienation present such complexity that it is extremely difficult even for relatives of the patient to make sure of the principal influence under which the malady develops. It often occurs that what they regard as the efficient cause, is in reality only a secondary effect."

was the true history of the tragic case of one of the most brilliant men, by nature, I have ever known. But how does this theory account for the phenomenon of apparently drunken insanity here, in excess of such insanity there? My answer is, that from the causes I have already indicated, there is more insanity, in the aggregate, among our people, in proportion to numbers, than there is in the other sections. And the mistake being often made, of supposing drink to be its cause, where, in a large class of cases, it is rather the antecedent than the cause, we are, therefore, reported to have twice as much mental disease created by drink, when in fact we consume very much less drink to create it.

Let me give a further proof. The whole number of deaths recorded as caused by " Insanity," occurring in the years 1859, '60, found in the volume on " Mortality" prepared by Dr. Jarvis himself, and printed by order of Congress, was 452 in all the States. There were other insane persons who died, but whose deaths were immediately caused by other diseases superinduced. But of those who died from insanity, the proportion was twice as great in the north-eastern as in the north-western districts, twice as great as in the south-west, more than twice as great as in the south-east, and more than twice as great as in the tier of States comprising Ohio, Indiana, Illinois, Iowa and Kansas, and a great deal larger than in other districts, except in California. It is plain, therefore, that insanity is a disease, which, in its various manifestations, appears in larger ratio, and is fatal to more people, in the north-east, than in most other portions of the country. The excess in California is truly ascribed by Dr. Jarvis, (on page 243 of the Census Volume of "Mortality,") to " the excitement and oppressive anxieties, and the great and sudden changes of fortune among many of the people." Applying the same rule to the north-east, we find the cause of our greater ratio of insanity, in the commercial fortuities, the speculative adventures, the hurrying, crowded, excited, anxious habits of manufacturing and commercial cities, the excessive nervous exposure of artists, poets, lawyers, and all persons of overtasked brains, distinguishing our civilization. Insanity, indeed, is peculiarly " a feature of developing civilization."* It is thus described by our own Board of State Charities, and with learned emphasis. Besides, the bad sanitary condition of narrow lanes and alleys, where certain classes abide and die before their time, among

* Second Annual Report of the Massachusetts Board of State Charities, p. ciii. (Mass. Pub. Doc. 1865, No. 19.)

the denser populations, piles up another agony in the accumulation of human woe, of which madness is one of the mysterious signs. Thus our sum total of insanity is relatively greater than for example, that of the West. But this excess of our own insanity compared with population, furnishes no reason why the peculiar form of madness incident to drunkenness shóuld be still further increased and be twice as common in proportion to our whole volume of insanity. But, if this appearance is not merely superficial; if it is real; and if in Massachusetts, in fact, more than twice as many people go mad from drink as in other places known to be less abstinent, I leave the unexplained phenomenon to be disposed of by others. I believe the explanation to be, (and these statistics concur in proving it,) that drunkenness is oftentimes a *manifestation* of independently existing mania, mistaken, by superficial observation, for the *cause*.

These leaves of Dr. Jarvis have still further value. They confirm, by the weight of his opinion, the tables of mortality in the Census. It had been contended on behalf of the remonstrants, that such returns could deserve little trust; that the deaths from " *delirium tremens*," and from " intemperance," and from " insanity," as returned and tabulated, could not be true. But Dr. Jarvis himself exhibits now just such tables, which can be drawn only from such sources. It had been gravely urged by one of the strongest and most intelligent of their witnesses, that the mortality from intemperance was *fifty thousand* a year in the United States! And, when I called attention to the proof, that the deaths from " *delirium tremens* " were in 1860 but 575, that those from " intemperance " were returned as 931 in all, that the mortality from " diseases of the brain " (regarded by their own physiological authorities as the great seat of the diseases generated by alcohol,) was returned at only 5,726 in the aggregate, and when I vainly begged to know how the estimate of the witness was made, my facts and figures were received with incredulity. Now the whole sum of mortality in the whole country, from all causes, was less than 374,000 in 1860, of which number by the theory of the witness in question, about one in seven was due to drink. But, one of the leaves presented by Dr. Jarvis, on the stand, shows that, even in Boston, (bad as she is represented by the pro-hibitionists,) in the dark decade from the year 1820 to 1830, the mortality was but 309 from intemperance, to 10,000 of all known causes, or about three deaths from intemperance, out of 100 from all causes. And it also exhibits a descent, during the last five and forty years, from even that ratio, until during the fifteen years ending with the year 1865, there was a ratio of 85.9 to the 10,000, or *less than one to one hundred.* And this is Boston, bearing as she must, not only the sins of her own people, but of strangers, of a large mass of entirely exceptional persons, dying under exceptional circumstances, and not representing at all the average health or the general sobriety.

In Lowell, Dr. Jarvis's tables show that in the decade ending with 1851, the mortality from intemperance was but 56.9 to the 10,000 deaths, or little more than half of one to an hundred; and that, as in Boston, so there also, *without enforcing prohibition, but by the moral self-restraint of the people*, that species of mortality has still further diminished and has for the past fifteen years, been at less than half the former ratio, or about one-quarter of one death from intemperance to one hundred deaths from all causes. The same tables show, that taking all the counties but Suffolk, out of 81,473 deaths from all known causes, during the years 1861 to 1864, there were 298 from intemperance, or the ratio of 36.5 to the 10,000, less than four-tenths of one to the hundred deaths. And the seven counties of Barnstable, Berkshire, Franklin, Hampshire, Hampden, Dukes and Nantucket, from an aggregate of 113 deaths from intemperance, in the decade of 1841 to 1850, out of 24,684 from all known causes, fell down, in the next decade, to 123 deaths from intemperance, out of 39,991 from all causes. The former decade gave 45.8 to the 10,000, and the latter but 30.7 to the 10,000.

And all this proof of the conquering power of ideas, of reason and moral sentiment, to reform *abuses*, has accumulated during a time when the *use* is more general, and when the cause of true temperance is demoralized by a law on the statute book, constantly defied.

Accidents in 1860, from the discharge of fire-arms alone, destroyed 741 lives ; railway accidents, 599 ; accidental poison, 950 ; while the aggregate of accidental causes was fatal to 18,090 persons, an army corps in number. Even " old age " which is intended to include only those who die from exhaustion of vital force from protracted use of life, without any disease or organic lesion—attended 4,899 men and 5,988 women, or 10,887 in all, to the last repose of our poor humanity.

Figures may be thought to be apparently in favor of the health and sobriety of the country populations as against the city. But it should be observed that the progress of sobriety has been as great in the city as in the country, notwithstanding the exceptional disadvantages of crowded quarters and floating classes.

I must afford time for one proof that the great body of young and middle-aged men in Boston, in spite of all the supposed temptations of the metropolis, are not behind their rural neighbors in the physical qualities of manhood. Of the 29,194 men 'drafted by the United States in the summer of 1863, and of the 9,830 who volunteered under the stimulus of high bounties and the short term of service, during the last eight months of the war, being 39,024 in all, there were rejected by the surgeons, 14,827. These two bodies are fairly representative—the first because raised on an equal draft, the second because stimulated by the same enthusiasms, and by State and town bounties, both large and similar. (No calculation covering the aggregate volume of physical examinations and the results, in this Commonwealth, during the whole war, is accessible.)

The number of these men, drafted or recruited and examined, in the two representative districts to which Boston belongs, (viz.: the third and fourth,) was 12,741, and the number in the other eight districts was 26,283. Of those examined in the two Boston districts, the number rejected by the surgeons was 3,946, or 310 to each thousand examined; while, of those examined in the other eight districts, the rejections were 10,881, or 414 to each thousand,—thus exhibiting about three-fourths as many rejections to the thousand in the Boston districts as are found in the residue of the Commonwealth.

Mr. Chairman: The proof is clear that neither mortality nor insanity, nor any of the fatal exhibitions of intemperance, bad as they are, afford any ground for panic, or " military necessity in legislation." But one of the advocates before this Committee, and many of the witnesses, have declared they meant " *to put it through*," to " overcome obstacles," to " remember that Massachusetts can do whatever she undertakes." Another advocate, perhaps the most eloquent of them all, and not the least imprudent, has declared in public, that they intend " to exhaust the ingenuity of the Yankee mind" in devising measures to compel the due subordination of their opponents.

But, if gentlemen believe that a standing menace, a perpetual sneer, the denial of sincerity or conscientiousness, the positive accusation of being moved by appetite, or by gain, the habitual affectation of superiority, both of rights and of character (with which these petitioners, their advocates and witnesses have been met and opposed by persons on the stand and off of it, by public speech, and through the " prohibitory " press) will ultimately avail, when the results of this hearing shall have been spread before " the Yankee mind "—they have misconceived its intelligence, and its fairness, the spirit of liberty, refinement and progress.

Whenever you begin this work of enforced conformity, there are perils in your way little imagined. It is of no use to beg the question, by the short method of stigmatizing opponents as criminals, or as upholders of criminality. There is now *proved* to be—what certain gentlemen affected to doubt before— a powerful, convinced, intellectual, revered and noble body of people, numerically strong, and not surpassed by any, in aught that yields weight, dignity and influence, denying the dogmas of the prohibitionists, challenging the philosophy of their movement, the fitness of their methods, their consistency with liberty, with progress, and with the ultimate good. A denunciatory harangue, impugning the character of a private citizen, or the motives of a sworn and responsible magistrate, will not longer avail against this array. If, against the judgment of the best men you insist on this coercion, and trample on convictions as well as rights, let me remind you that the same argument of *necessity* may be used to strike where now you little dream. Stay a moment. Take this very illustration of insanity again. The census report* gives a table prepared by Dr. Butler, of the " Hartford Retreat," exhibiting the whole number of cases in four leading hospitals, in which the causes of insanity have been noted. There were 7,591 cases, in all. Of these, 2,253 were found due to " ill health," and 812 to " intemperance." Thus there was found nearly three times as much statistical proof of a necessity to take under guardianship the whole course of domestic life and personal habit, physical and moral, for the protection of the community against suffering from the madness of sick people, as against that of the other class. Nor is that all. If " intemperance " caused the madness of 812, so " *religious excitement* " came next in the order, and crazed 740 more. What will you do with these? You admit that you have no right to restrain or appoint the use of stimulants by the citizen. He may use them in his diet, as well as for his medicine, if he *can*. But, you will prevent his *getting* them, by forbidding any one to sell them, unless as a public agent. And you will direct the public agent to make inquisition of the use intended, and to refuse them if wanted for a dietetic purpose. Thus, by indirection,

---

* See " Introduction," to Volume on " Population," of the Census Report, of 1860, p. lxxxix.

—not deemed honorable as between gentlemen, not deemed fair dealing as between merchants, not permitted by the Gospel, which enjoins that your " yea " shall mean *yea*, and your " nay " shall mean *nay*,— your law aims to do, and its supporters make a virtue of trying to do, what it *purports* to omit, what it *pretends* to avoid. It, in fact, undertakes to get into the household, control the domestic economy and the diet of the citizen, by a sumptuary law artfully worded. The supreme court may not be able to reach and overrule it. But, there is " a higher law," by which it is inevitably rejudged.

If the legislature can do thus, then why not also lay hands on the promoters of " religious excitement? " Do you reply that people have the right to think according to conscience, on religion? True; and so you *say* they have a right to select their own diet. Suppose you compare the number of people made crazy by " religious excitement " with the number of sinners returned as converted, and on comparing them you find the ratio of that insanity greater than the ratio alcoholic insanity bears to the aggregate of temperate drinkers, what is to hinder the application of your argument from " military necessity? " Why not admit the right to *think*, but deny to some classes the dangerous right to *preach?* Does the constitution hinder? Then why not try "the ingenuity of the Yankee mind," by agitating to amend the constitution, to rid us of such an evil? Some of the denominations might not object, if they are not wedded to the *idea* of *liberty*. It might be found that the confessional, the absolution, and the sacraments of salvation, offered by the Church of Rome, give such peace of mind that its ministers prevent insanity and create none. It might be urged that the denominations styled "Liberal" neither alarm nor console, and therefore, if they do no good, do no harm. It might be set up that Calvinism distracts the understanding, scares the imagination, and leaves an awful doubt forever hanging over the tremendous problem of election and reprobation; that Arminianism is exciting, noisy, and guilty of placing an overwhelming responsibility on the sinner's mind, since it leaves everlasting issues to depend on his working out his own salvation. Romanism, then, together with the "Liberals," might be left by the law in substantially undisputed possession of the field—as the "State agency" appointed to preach down insanity and lower the taxes now wrung from our pockets to support 740 people a year driven mad by religious emotions and measures which they could not "assimilate" nor "digest."

But, suppose, for the moment, that our part of
the immense trade in alcoholics,—of which ninety
million gallons were manufactured in this country in
1860,—could be taken by legislative machinery out
of *commerce* and put into *politics*, so that the governor, or his agent, the liquor commissioner, should be
the only lawful wholesale dealer, besides the import-
ers selling only their original packages, which could
never be broken for sale, nor sold again, unless by
the commissioner. And, for all the myriad uses of
our diversified industry into which alcohol enters, (as
it does enter in almost every conceivable way through
manufactures and the arts, being found at last in solid,
as well as fluid forms, in our lights, in the gases, and
in most medicines, at some stage or other of their
preparation,) suppose for the moment that only the
local agents of the government should actually sell it
by retail at all. Remember, that there is an actual
demand in the whole country, by the public taste, good
and bad, for at least forty million gallons to drink.
Alongside of this demand, in ordinary times, there is,
with our present population and under wise taxation,
a demand for some fifty million gallons more for other
uses agreed to be legitimate. When politics have
got the monopoly of the latter business, they will
not wait long before grasping at the former. The

business, (for ends acknowledged legitimate,) will then have swollen in the hands of the commissioner and his friends,—who manufacture and import for him, who sell or consign to him, to whom he is indebted, or under obligations,—to the proportions of a vast overshadowing monopoly, of which the profits would belong to a few, represented in every hamlet, on every hillside and river bank of Massachusetts, by an army of local agents in correspondence and in fatal relations with the " head centre " of the monopoly at Boston, who would " pull the wires" felt in every town and district caucus, and would " log-roll " with every similar enterprise aimed at the subversion of local and personal independence. Strong in the power of such a gigantic " machine " invented in a spasm of " Yankee ingenuity," impudent with ill-gotten wealth, and bloated by greedy ambition,—like the two daughters of the horse-leech, (in the Proverbs) they will perpetually cry " *give! give!* " Do you believe in the virtuous self-denial of such an unnatural alliance between trade and politics, consummated in defiance of the principles of political economy, maintained by subverting ancient safeguards of liberty; created by a statute which—professed to be made in the interest of a high moral testimony against the sale of even wines not less than spirits distilled—

allows the manufacture of New England Rum by the wholesale, to be sent abroad to all the earth, and among our missionaries to the heathen, without hindrance or rebuke? I warn honest gentlemen, who desire that the traffic in these dangerous and seductive, yet needful and indispensable liquids, shall be kept within the reach of regulation, wherever order and decorum demand the intervention of government, and the government can rightly intervene,—I warn them that your machinery may be found, at last, more powerful than the inventors. You may yet find, that after political corruption shall have subsidized the party leaders, and demoralized the party, dedicated by its name, and consecrated by its life to *Republican* liberty, it will reveal itself in all the hideous proportions of the Devil, though now wearing a shining robe. I forewarn you of the day surely coming, unless you recede, when the monopoly you are striving to create, greedy for more gain and more power, anxious to increase and not to diminish its sales, will " run the machine " in the interest of unlimited consumption by our own people, as well as by the heathen. When that day comes, it will be found that your machinery, the motive power of which will be a stream of Rum, swollen by all the affluents of commerce, will have a wheel large enough for the stream, and that the whole stream will be turned on the wheel. I pray you to avoid trying the fatal experiment to see whether in that day, and until a new revolution shall break the chain you now are forging, Massachusetts will own the Trade in Rum, or the Monopolists of the Trade will own Massachusetts, selling *what* they please, *as* they please, *to whom* they please, limiting their business only by the fatality of their beverages. *The only safety of " the machine " is found in the fact that it never will be made to work.*

We propose, Mr. Chairman, a scheme which will liberate the Commonwealth, and give scope to the religious and virtuous encouragement, whether of Temperance or of Abstinence. Enact a law leaving the wholesale liquor trade with commerce, where it belongs. Provide for assay and inspection, to protect the people from imposition. If you can allow men to distil liquors for wholesale, for the uses of arts and manufactures, as now you do, there is no pretext for interference with the product of importation. Permit the municipalities to license taverners to furnish to their guests, in their rooms, or on their tables with their meals, whatever beverages, as well as whatever meat, they demand and the markets afford, according to the customs of social and domestic life. Allow them also to license victuallers to sell fermented beverages, in like manner, with the meals of their guests, and allow grocers to retail in packages conveniently small for domestic or culinary use and for employment in manufactures and the arts ; and, in the name of ordinary fairness and common reason, grant the petition of the College of Pharmacy.

Having adopted a scheme which looks to the discontinuance of public tippling places, or saloons, or bars, of all kinds, *surround the licensees by such police regulations as may be, to restrain that abuse.* Your regulation of the retail, trade will then securely repose on the clear social right to maintain order and public decorum, endangered by bar-rooms and tippling shops, where dangerous and seductive beverages are offered neither as medicine, nor as diet, to the chance crowds of the hour, tempted by each other to drink without appetite, to linger without motive, and to revel without enjoyment,

"Where laughter is not mirth, nor thought the mind,
Nor words a language, nor even men mankind."

If you fear that local influences may indulge individuals at the risk of the public, then give to the judges of the Court of Probate and of the Superior Court, sitting in Chambers, jurisdiction on summary hearing, upon sworn complaint of any selectman or alderman, or of the Constable of the Commonwealth, to annul any license which the municipal authorities refuse to annul, on proof to the judge's satisfaction that its holder has broken the law or the conditions of his license.

Do this fairly, with no effort to reduce the people to inconvenient straits in the pursuit of what in their own judgment they need.

Under the forms of republican legislation, do not, in the short-sighted service of morality without Faith, seek to play either the tyrant or the pedagogue.

In the words of John Quincy Adams, whose austere virtue and greatness made him for years the representative statesman of New England, uttered in addressing the Temperance Society of Norfolk County, five and twenty years ago :—

" *Forget not* [*I pray you*] *the rights of personal freedom.* * * * Self-government is the foundation of all our political and social institutions, and it is by self-government alone that the law of temperance can be enforced. * * * Seek not to enforce upon [your brother,] by legislative enactment, that virtue which he can possess only by the dictate of his own conscience and the energy of his own will."

Abiding by such principles, you will put an end to the antagonism between the government, and the people who consume. You will have preserved your own dignity, undertaken your own duties, and recognized their rights. With all the methods and forces of the present laws, and of the existing decisions, at your command for the punishment of those who sell without license, or in breach of one, you will stand in a position a hundred-fold stronger than you do to-day, or than you ever stood before. Recognizing the retail trade in liquors as having an exceptional side, and therefore requiring a certain police supervision which every town may not desire to undertake, we do not ask it to be forced upon any town against its will. While the means of purchase for certain uses are furnished through the agency, and while the competition of other towns exists, and the power to institute the same competition exists there also, a given town may prefer to exclude it. The fatal monopoly I have described will then be impossible; and the right of the citizen will be preserved to buy *somewhere* in the Commonwealth those things he needs, in his own judgment, for his family and for himself.

It is puerile to inveigh against this plan, as making the " criminal laws of the Commonwealth " subject to municipal interference. That is substituting an adjective for an argument. These laws are only

128

" criminal " because they are made so, or called so. They are properly police regulations (often essentially municipal,) concerning the distribution of certain articles of merchandise, universally admitted to have their proper uses, needful to be bought and sold, but liable to abuse. One breaking those regulations is liable to indictment or complaint. In that sense, they are criminal laws. But, there always have been other laws, the violation of which subjects one to criminal procedure, as for misdemeanor, just as these do, which are subordinated to municipal administration, and which even owe their very being to the will of the respective cities and towns.

But, do you profess that these prohibitory laws were enacted in the exercise of your best discretion ; and that in your judgment the case for a change has not been made out ? I then beg to meet that position by the counter position taken by some of the ablest and wisest men in Massachusetts, in testimony before this Committee, *denying the right of government thus to pass into the domestic and private sphere.*

If there is a man born to speak the English tongue, who combines high integrity, great attainments, practical wisdom and theoretical statesmanship, with faith in, and devotion to, free government, and the elevation of the humble, that man—one of the truest friends of

America in the Old World—is *John Stuart Mill*. And thus he wrote :—

"There are in our own day, gross usurpations upon the liberty of private life actually practised, and still greater ones threatened, with some expectation of success; and opinions proposed which assert an unlimited right in the public not only to prohibit by law everything which it thinks wrong, but in order to get at what it thinks wrong, to prohibit any number of things which it admits to be innocent.

"Under the name of preventing intemperance, the people of one English colony, and of nearly half the United States, have been interdicted by law from making any use whatever of fermented drinks, except for medical purposes; for prohibition of their sale is in fact, as it is intended to be, prohibition of their use. * * * The infringement complained of is not on the liberty of the seller, but on that of the buyer and consumer; since the State might just as well forbid him to drink wine, as purposely make it impossible for him to obtain it. The secretary, however, [of the English "Alliance"] says, 'I claim, as a citizen, a right to legislate whenever my social rights are invaded by the social act of another.' And now for the definition of these 'social rights.' 'If anything invades my social rights, certainly the traffic in strong drink does. It destroys my primary right of security, by constantly creating and stimulating social disorder. It invades my right of equality, by deriving a profit from the creation of a misery I am taxed to support. It impedes my right to free moral and intellectual development, by surrounding my path with dangers, and by weakening and demoralizing society, from which I have a right to claim mutual aid and intercourse.' A theory of 'social

17

rights,' the like of which probably never before found its way into distinct language, being nothing short of this, that it is the absolute social right of every individual that every other individual shall act in every respect exactly as he ought; that whosoever fails thereof in the smallest particular, violates my social right, and entitles me to demand from the legislature the removal of the grievance. So monstrous a principle is far more dangerous than any single interference with liberty; there is no violation of liberty which it would not justify; it acknowledges no right to any freedom whatever except perhaps to that of holding opinions in secret, without ever disclosing them."*

I appeal also to William von Humboldt, the friend of Schiller and of Goethe, a statesman, a scholar, an ambassador of Prussia, a minister of State, who re-organized public instruction and gave to the Prussian system much of the eminence it enjoys, whose forecast attempted to consolidate Germany against the first Napoleon, as Bismarck has, more than a half century later, consolidated it against Napoleon III., and of whom it was said by Talleyrand, that there were not three men in Europe of his ability :—

"The State may content itself with exercising the most watchful vigilance on every unlawful project, and defeating it before it has been put into execution: or, advancing further, it may prohibit actions which are harmless in themselves, but which tempt to the commission of crime, or

* Mill on Liberty, pp. 170-73.

afford opportunities for resolving upon criminal actions. This latter policy, again, tends to encroach on the liberty of the citizens ; manifests a distrust on the part of the State which not only operates hurtfully on the character of the citizens, but goes to defeat the very end in view. * * * All that the State may do, without frustrating its own end, and without encroaching on the freedom of its citizens, is, therefore, restricted to the former course ; that is, the strictest surveillance of every trangression of the law, either already committed or only resolved on ; and as this cannot properly be called preventing the causes of crime, I think I may safely assert that this prevention of criminal actions is wholly foreign to the State's proper sphere of activity.*

One of the latest and best expositions of the "Rationale of Government and Legislation" is found in a recent volume bearing that title, by Lord Wrottesley, in which, without pretension to novelty of reasoning, (which would, perhaps, be a demerit,) he has presented the results arrived at by the best modern writers on the philosophy of government.

The following propositions so clearly express the conclusions of reason and experience, that I am prepared to adopt and to proclaim them as the voice of authority.

" *First.* Laws should never be passed which either cannot be executed, or of which the execution is so difficult

* Sphere and Duties of Government, (W. v. Humboldt,) p. 171,

that the temptation to neglect their observance is likely to surmount the fear of the punishment.

"*Second.* Laws should never be passed forbidding acts which, in the opinion of a large proportion of the educated members of the community, are in themselves innocent.

"*Third.* Laws should not generally be passed which, though good in themselves, either too much *anticipate* public opinion, or are hostile to the deliberately-formed sentiments of a large majority of the population of any country.

"*Fourth.* No attempt should be made to reform the moral conduct of society by the enactments of positive law,—that is, to make men good and virtuous by Act of Parliament."

The venerable and reverend Doctor Leonard Withington, in the dawn of this attempt at enforced conformity, sounded the note of remonstrance, with prophetic wisdom.

"I desire to bear my solemn testimony, and to say that though I have seen frequent attempts, I never knew any good to come from such legislation. I have seen men exasperated by it but never reformed. So it ever has been, and so it ever will be, until nature itself is changed. I was in Connecticut when attempts were made to enforce the observance of the Sabbath by law. I saw hypocrisy, power, passion, haughtiness, indignation, force, resistance, commands, threats, cursing; but I saw no promotion of meekness among Christians or repentance among sinners. The contest was long and the fruits were bitter. Long did it take to teach the sober part of the community a simple truth. *What the law could not do, in that it was weak through the flesh, God, sending his own Son in the likeness of sinful flesh, and for sin, condemned sin in the flesh, that the righteousness of the law might be fulfilled in us who walk not after the flesh, but after the spirit.*"

" If any person can devise a plan for prohibitory legislation on the sale of intoxicating drinks, not involving the greatest inconsistency even in the very scheme, then I will acknowledge he has done what surpasses the utmost flights of my imagination. This very plan must be a square wheel made to roll. But how absurd 'it is to expect success in the execution, when you cannot even devise consistency in the design! You launch a vessel full of holes and expect her not to sink."

" Remember that some are drunkards because they are poor; some because they are idle; some because they are disappointed; some because they are ignorant; some from an unhappy nervous system; and all because they are not Christians. Reflect that there are indirect as well as direct efforts to oppose this evil; and that sometimes the indirect efforts are the most effectual. Is a man idle, endeavor to employ him; is he ignorant, instruct him; is he disappointed, point him to the true source of consolation; and, above all things, beware how you lord it over his faults, or play the Pharisee over his vices. Recollect that intemperance is seldom an insulated vice; it grows up in wide combinations; and you are never fitted to engage in the subject of reforming it until you have sounded the depths from which it springs."

IT is urged by many good men that spirits and wines are so alluring, that health and morals require teetotalism as the only safeguard. That while there is evidence, by which many men otherwise trustworthy are convinced, in favor of a certain, temperate, dietetic use by some people, yet the moral dangers to the mass are such that teetotalism ought not only to be universally volunteered, but that it ought to receive the vindication of the Statute book, and the moral support of the legislature.

The whole argument involves one of the oldest of human errors; so entirely human that it has no shadow of countenance from the religion of the New Testament. This world, in which while in the body we must abide, and this body in which the spirit dwells, have been felt by many philosophers and moralists, both Christian and heathen, to work a sad imprisonment of the celestial spirit. The immaculate purity of the spirit, soiled by any indulgence of the gross and material body, recedes from all human passion, and oftentimes from all intercourse with this tempting, dangerous, material world, to which alone, in the temptation of a simple fruit, hanging on one of the trees of Eden, is due our whole experience of woe and the awful mystery of evil. The Church has always been tolerant, the Church of Rome has sometimes been too indulgent, of this mysticism; while some of the Protestant sects, as well as of the societies in the Roman Church, have made it their vital principle. But it had its original expression in oriental philosophy, not in Christianity, nor even in Judaism.

When our Saviour came to the Jews, He found them mainly in these sects or divisions,—the Pharisees and the Sadducees. The latter, relatively small, maintained the law as written by Moses, denying the traditions of the Elders. They were rich, educated and influential, but cold, hard and unspiritual. The Pharisees were devoted to their religion, professed to live meanly, to despise delicacies, to venerate the Elders. But many of them, with ostentatious prayers, sacrificed the heart of humanity on the altar of ceremonious and hollow sanctity. Besides these, were the Essenes. They were very few, and were sincere, but narrow.

Doubtless recruited from the sect of Pharisees they held rather to their general views, which had an ascetic tendency. But, in a spirit of devout, self-denying, mystic yearning after God, they sought him in the ecstasies of contemplation, through exile, poverty and want; instead of facing the world, bearing its social burdens, risking its evils, temptations and woes. Although there were many observances pertaining to the flesh, ritually imposed upon the Jew, including many dietetic limitations, there was in the law of Moses no prohibition against drinking wine—

which was the intoxicating beverage of Palestine—save only the command to Aaron, and his posterity, (the priesthood,)* not to drink wine nor strong drink when going before the congregation, lest they might by accident put the clean for the unclean in the holy sacrifice of the tabernacle. There were stringent laws to maintain the purity of woman, and of the family descent. But, there was no suggestion in the law of Moses of a peculiar sanctity in a celibate life. The Jew was educated to believe marriage honorable, and a fruitful posterity a pride and blessing. But, there were occasionally men and women who assumed the vow of a Nazarite, (which word implies *separation*,) " to separate themselves unto the Lord, * * * from wine and strong drink," to eat nothing "made of the vine tree, from the kernel even to the husk;" not to permit the hair nor the beard to be shorn, to touch no dead body, nor to make themselves ritually unclean, for father, mother, brother, or sister, " during the days of their separation."† We read of a few persons devoted by their parents for life, while yet unborn, to this separation. Samson was one. · John the Baptist was another. He was sequestered from the world,

* Leviticus, chapter 10, v. 9, 10.
† Numbers, chapter 6, v. 2-21.

living a monkish, or a hermit, life, according to the ascetic notions of the Essenes, refusing alike to marry, to drink wine, or to live in conformity with the social life of Palestine.

Inspired by a sublime enthusiasm of prophecy, watching for the expected Messiah, (but unlike so many Jews, who looked for a conquering king, imagining Him as coming from Edom, with dyed garments from Bozrah, glorious in his apparel, travelling in the greatness of his strength, having trodden the wine-press alone, now trampling the people in his anger,*) John,—stationed by the ford of Jordan, where the waters had divided before the ark, amid the rich vegetation and grateful shade of this spot of romantic beauty, where so often he is described in painting as surrounded by multitudes and performing the initiatory rite of salvation,—recognized and proclaimed "the Lamb of God, who taketh away the sins of the World."

The Messiah accepted the recognition and the baptism of John. But though He did this honor to the prophet, and accepted his emblem of the inward purifying of the soul, and of the spiritual and celestial character of his own coming, (as contrasted with some fierce apparition of triumphant wrath,) the Saviour

---

* Isaiah, chapter 63, v. 1-3.

18

immediately made clear his own disagreement with the dogmas of the Essenes, and the notions of asceticism.

Soon after his baptism, there was a marriage-feast. Invited to attend, He joined the festivity. In compliance with the wishes of his Mother, the wine having failed, Jesus, by miracle, changed 'water into wine, and sent it to the master of the feast. "Thus Jesus performed his first miracle at Cana, in Galilee, and *manifested his glory.*"* By these two actions, of emphatic significance,—that is, by attending the marriage-feast and making the wine,— our Lord, with the utmost publicity, placed himself in unequivocal antagonism to the asceticism of Naza-rite and Essene, prevented his baptism from being mistaken for any profession of adhesion to the sect, the dogmas, or the practices of John; sanctioned the domestic tie, which the Essene contemned; the use of the beverage, which the Nazarite rejected; and the friendly enjoyment of innocent festivity.

On no other theory can we understand the meaning of his joining the feast, or working the miracle. In the very hour of festivity the dreadful future of his Passion was presented to his soul. He sympathized with the social joy of others; but He was sad himself.

* Gospel of St. John, chapter 2, v. 11. Norton's translation.

Nor can we regard the miracle as wrought either to display his power, or simply for the hilarity of the feast. It would be to degrade the character of our Lord, and imagine motives to which He never yielded in the use of his heavenly gifts. If we perceive in his conduct the evident testimony He bore against opinions sincerely held by John, but of which He would not even *seem* to be the adherent, we shall better understand the spirit of the occasion, and the true character of our Lord, and we shall learn what Paul, the apostle, learned perhaps from the story of the same miracle, (while Peter needed its revelation in vision,) that " *The kingdom of God is not meat and drink.*"

Had Jesus been accessible to ordinary motives, He would have adopted, or at least indulged, asceticism. It would have given Him a party at the beginning of his career. It would have helped Him to defy, or to puzzle, the Pharisees, and to turn their weapons. But He was absorbed in the infinite purpose of a mission which included all human nature, all times, all places, and all circumstances of men.

When the great Apostle to the Gentiles was a prisoner in Rome, the Christians in Colosse, one of the Phrygian cities, sent Epaphras with messages of comfort to Paul. He returned home with " the Epistle to the Colossians" in reply. The Greeks had, long before the Gospel, introduced their philosophy into Asia Minor. And, in Phrygia, the doctrines of both Plato and Pythagoras found many disciples; against some of the opinions of both of whom the Epistle is in part directed. Besides these, were the teachings of Judaisers, endeavoring to impress upon the Christians Mosaic observances. In order to attract those Christians who had been Platonists or Pythagoreans, it is supposed that the Judaisers tried to convince them that those philosophers had themselves been taught by the writings of Moses. Thus, through Judaisers, of the strictly ritualistic, or formalist and purely pharisaic school, and through others of the Essene, or purely ascetic school, and through Pythagoreans who carried out the doctrine of transmigration of souls to the logical conclusion of rejecting the flesh of animals as food, the infant Christian church of Colosse was in peril of dogmatic demoralization. Here, Paul—like his Master in the beginning—turned his back upon the temptation so plainly set before him. He would not humor the peculiarities of any of these several schools, all of which, though from different origins, might have been combined in a common end of giving some formal expression to a higher life, in which Greek reason, Oriental mysticism and Jewish reverence for a divinely given ritual, could have rallied around Christianity as a common centre. But the poor prisoner bound in Rome, would not compromise one iota of the simplicity and grandeur of that lofty Faith, whose deeper meanings and universal application none among the Apostles knew so well. Therefore he commanded his converts to avoid alike an empty philosophy, the traditions of men, and the elements of this world, which are not according to Christ. Abjuring the theories of the Greeks and the Orientalists, the rites of Moses, the intercession of angels, he warned them to let no man (whether Greek or Jew, Essene, Nazarite or Pythagorean,) judge them in respect of *meats* or *drinks ;* of partaking animal food, or of drinking wine, in the temperate repast of Christian Liberty.*

While the great Apostle was willing,—in tenderness to a brother whose weakness demanded charity,—not to eat meat nor drink wine, if by eating or drinking he would lead to the misapprehension that he was recognizing idolatrous worship,† he placed that willingness wholly on the ground of an affectionate concession, *not at all on any ground of any form of asceticism.* Had it been proposed in the Christian church

* See, among other authorities on this whole subject, " Milman's History of Christianity," and " MacKnight on the Epistles."

† Romans, chapter 14.

to establish asceticism by creed or discipline, it would have aroused the utmost power reposing in the mightiest pen ever held by human hand.

It was left for Mohammed, as a measure of *real* "military necessity," by pretended revelation, to fulminate an interdict. Christianity, the only Religion "which is not naturally weakened by civilization," which "has traversed the lapse of ages, acquiring a new strength and beauty with each advance of civilization, and infusing its beneficent influence into every sphere of thought and action," * omitted asceticism wholly from its plan. It has led the conquering march of humanity, under the inspiration of its Founder, in obedience to immortal hope and celestial love ; subordinating passion and appetite, not by the law of a carnal commandment, but by the power of an endless life. The Gospel of Jesus preached and testified by apostles, evangelists, confessors and martyrs, descends to no comparison with the Koran of Mohammed, whose sword, succeeded by the torch of Omar, led the hordes of Islam to the slaughter of the unbelievers.†

* "Rationalism in Europe," by W. E. H. Lecky. Vol. i., pp. 311, 312. (American edition.)

† See, among other authorities, "Mohammed der Prophet," [Stuttgart. 1843,] by Gustav Weil, then assistant-librarian, since 1845 Professor of Oriental Languages in the University of Heidelberg. At page 140, the learned author says :—"The danger which Mohammed incurred from his followers addicting themselves to the use of wine, was probably the occasion of this prohibition." Also, "Essais sur l'histoire des Arabes," etc.,

How much the Mohammedan interdict has been worth to the morality of *Persia*, (whatever was its value under military organization, on the march or in camp,) may be learned from the testimony of both travellers and missionaries :—

"Prohibiting the use of wine to its followers, tends to restrict the manufacture to those places where the Jews, Americans, or Hindoos, form part of the population. But

[Paris, 1847,] by Armand Pierre Caussin de Perceval, Professor of Arabic in the College of France, vol. iii, page 122, where he says :—"According to the common opinion, it was during one of Mohammed's *sieges* in the territory of Medina, that he published the verses of the Koran which interdict wine and games of chance to the faithful."

Frederick von Schlegel, in his Lectures on the Philosophy of History, (Robertson's Translation, Bohn's edition, page 327,) suggests a second motive of Mohammed in making the prohibition. He says :—"Even the prohibition of wine was perhaps not so much intended for a moral precept, which, considered in that point of view, would be far too severe, as for answering a *religious* design of the founder ; for he might hope that the express condemnation of a liquid *which forms an essential element of the Christian sacrifice*, would necessarily recoil on *that sacrifice* itself, and thus raise an insuperable barrier between *his creed* and the religion of *Christ.*" This motive of Mohammed receives corroboration from the fact of his desire to proselyte from among the *Jews*, and from the consideration, (to which, however, Schlegel does not refer,) that the prohibition was likely to be one not altogether unacceptable to Jews, by reason of its confirmation of the antithesis between the Hebrew religion and the Christian religion on just this very point of the use of wine,—the only prohibition of its use by the Mosaic law being in connection with the religious rites of sacrifice, (Leviticus, c. 10, v. 9, 10.) (See also page 128 of this Argument.) Whereas it was precisely in the offering of the most significant Christian sacrament, (i. e., the Lord's Supper,) that its use was expressly ordained by Jesus, (Matthew, c. 26, v. 27. Mark, c. 14, v. 23.) And it is most remarkable, that while Moses forbade wine only to the priest, and then only when going "into the tabernacle of the congregation," Christianity enjoins the use of wine in the only sacrament which is universally administered at the altar and in the sanctuary. So deep is the Christian feeling in this precise relation of its use to the ceremonies of our religion, that the sale of wine for sacramental purposes is the only kind of sale which, by our prohibitory law, is free to all persons, at all places, and on all occasions.

the Persians have always been less scrupulous observers of this precept of the Koran than the other Mussulmans; and several of their kings, unable to resist the temptation, or conceiving themselves above the law, have set an example of drunkenness, which has been very generally followed by their subjects. * * * At present, many persons indulge secretly in wine and generally to intemperance; as they can imagine no pleasure in its use, unless it produce the full delirium of intoxication. They flatter themselves, however, that they diminish the sin by drinking only such as is made by infidels. * * * The Jews and Americans prepare wine on purpose for the Mohammedans by adding lime, hemp and other ingredients, to increase its pungency and strength : for the wine that soonest intoxicates is accounted the best, and the lighter and more delicate kinds are held in no estimation among the adherents of the prophet." *

Its moral influence on *Turkey*, I leave to the description of Lord Bacon, who styles Turkey—

"A cruel Tyranny, bathed in the blood of their emperors upon every succession ; a heap of vassals and slaves ; no nobles, no gentlemen, no freemen, no inheritance of land, no stirp of ancient families ; a people that is without natural affection, and as the scripture saith, that *regardeth not the desires of women;* and without piety or care toward their children ; a nation without morality, without letters,

---

* History of Ancient and Modern Wines. London, 1824.
See, also, Travels in Georgia and Persia, by Sir R. Kerr Porter, Vol. i., p. 348. Voyages de Chardin, Tom. ii., p. 67.
And, also, "Eight Years in Persia," by Rev. Justin Perkins, (missionary,) pp. 226, 227, and 402.

arts or sciences; that can scarce measure an acre of land or an hour of the day; base and sluttish in buildings, diet, and the like; and in a word, a very reproach of human society."*

The influence of entire abstinence upon all the different Mohammedan nations and races, to the extent the Mohammedan superstition has enforced it on the devout, I leave to the able writer of the article on "Food," in the Encyclopædia Brittanica.

" Many men, as the natives of Bengal and other countries, live entirely upon vegetables; and others, as the Esquimaux, altogether upon animal food, while most examples of the human species use a mixed diet of animal and vegetable matter; and the majority of people find it most convenient to obtain a portion of their supply of carbon from fermented drinks, or from drinks distilled from such. The number of people who abstain from fermented drinks, however, proves that the requisite amount of carbon may be obtained from saccharine or oleaginous compounds, the deficiency being in general, probably, made up from the latter. *There appears, nevertheless, to be little doubt but that, in order to attain the full perfection of the mental and bodily faculties, an admixture of animal and vegetable articles of food is essential; and also that a portion of the carbonaceous supply should be derived from alcoholic drinks.* Those who live almost entirely upon animal food become stunted in growth and liable to the ravages of scurvy, and their mental and moral faculties are blunted and sensual; those who consume only

† Lord Bacon's Works, (Boston edition,) Vol. xiii., p. 198, " Touching a Holy War."

vegetables are generally inactive and listless, and incapable of either active bodily or mental labor ; *and independently of other objections, there is reason to fear that the offspring of those who abstain entirely from fermented drinks, become in a generation or two enervated in mind and body. It is probably in this last mentioned manner that the decadence of the different Mohammedan nations and races is to be accounted for, at least in part.*" *

If you could enforce the outward observance of apparent conformity on a cowering and hypocritical population of unwilling subjects, judge you, by the testimony of Dr. Clarke, and of the ministers of religion, who know full well the workings of this law in the secret places, the devastation you will carry in its train. I desire, above all things, to bring the evil to the surface. It is safer on the skin than at the heart or in the brain. And bad as is the unguarded use of " rebellious liquors," it is safer—a hundred times safer—to bear with it, until it can be met by curing the inward disease of which drunkenness is a manifestation, rather than to push the determined consumers of narcotics to the terrible alternative of opium.

Literature is full of testimonies against such legislation. You find them in essays, in speeches, in history, uttered by Cromwell, by Milton, by Burke, by Macaulay,

* Encyclopædia Brittanica, (8th edition); Article "Food ; " subdivision, " The Principles of Dietetics ; " Vol. ix., p. 768.

and I know not how many besides. " Though you take from a covetous man all his treasure," says Milton, " he has one jewel left, ye cannot bereave him of his covetousness. Banish all objects of lust, shut up all youth into the severest discipline that can be exercised in any hermitage, ye cannot make them chaste that came not thither so. * * * Look how much we expel of sin, so much we expel of virtue. * * * This justifies the high providence of God, who, though he commands us temperance, justice, continence, yet pours out before us even to profuseness, all desirable things. * * * Why should we then affect a rigor contrary to the manner of God and of Nature." *

Mr. Chairman and Gentlemen, I have spoken boldly, as one of the advocates of thirty thousand voters of Massachusetts, who, without noise or observation, memorialized the General Court. Their opinions have been illustrated by more than one hundred witnesses, from all quarters of the Commonwealth. They are of nearly all professions and callings, men of learned pursuits and those devoted to the cares of busy life,

---

* See " Treasures from the Prose Writings of Milton," (by Ticknor & Fields,) passages from the " Areopagitica," the " Defence of the People of England," etc., pp. 112, 114, 115, 136, 158, and 345–6.

——Burke's Speeches, etc., (Little & Brown's Ed.,) Vol. v., pp. 163, 164.

——Macaulay's History of England, 5th Vol., c. 23, p. 41. (Harper's octavo edition.)

scholars, clergymen and statesmen, cultivators in the various sciences, and of wide renown, men of venerable years, and those of younger age. They are of the metropolis, the interior, the mountains of Berkshire, the valley of the Connecticut, the shores of Essex, the Islands and the Cape. They represent every phase of industry, of philanthropy and of wisdom. You heard, at the beginning, the eminent gentleman, my honored associate, [Hon. Linus Child,] whose life-long devotion to whatever is best in morality, in patriotism and religion, has made him a fit exemplar for all younger men of generous aspirations. When such as he have spoken, I might well have been content with silence. With a deep sense of the importance of this inquiry, and of the issue it involves, forgetting all things but the honor and welfare of our Commonwealth and her People, I dedicate this offering of gratitude and duty to the Future of Massachusetts.

1000822

Printed in Great Britain by
Amazon.co.uk, Ltd.,
Marston Gate.